Office
Relocation
Planner©

Office Relocation Planner©

THE Source for Planning, Managing and Executing Your Next Office Move – Today!

Karen Warner

VISION
Publications

Turning Your Business Vision into Reality

www.moveyouroffice.com

Office Relocation Planner©: THE Source for Planning, Managing and Executing Your Next Office Move – Today!

Contents

Introduction

Moving an office can be a wonderful thing. It's a chance to have a fresh start in a place whose look and location better represent your business and where it's headed. It's a chance to purge your workspace of clutter and a perfect opportunity to upgrade equipment of all types. It's a chance to reintroduce your company to the community and potentially attract some new business.

But if it's not done right, moving an office can also be a headache. Instead of serving as a morale booster for your employees, it can become a drain on both morale and productivity.

Office Relocation Planner is the guide to doing it right. It's the product of years of experience and research. I've taken what I've learned from the hundreds of commercial real estate clients I've served over the last two decades and combined it with insight gleaned from consultations with expert movers, space designers, IT professionals and more. The result is a comprehensive handbook walking you through every step of your move, from forming a relocation team and choosing a space to unpacking your boxes and filing claims for damage incurred during the move.

Figuring out the logistics and details of moving an office has the potential to become a full-time job, but chances are you've already got one of those. That's why my goal is to present you with everything you need to know in one place. Working with this guide, your relocation team can follow simple instructions to check off each task, leaving everyone free to spend most of their time running the business and taking care of clients.

I can't emphasize enough the importance of organization throughout the moving process. To help with that, I've included checklists, charts and worksheets throughout the book to keep your team on top of vendor quotes, necessary supplies and key details about the move. I've laid out a detailed timeline describing action steps you'll need to take beginning as soon as a year before your move date and continuing all the way through the days and weeks after you open your new doors to the public.

There are countless opportunities for costly missteps as you prepare for and execute your move, but with *Office Relocation Planner*, you'll be ready to charge past those common pitfalls and tackle the sometimes daunting process with efficiency and confidence.

You've taken the first step by reading *Office Relocation Planner*; now you're ready to make this office move your best move!

Best of luck,

Karen Warner

1 | Planning and Coordinating Your Office Move

Businesses move for a number of different reasons. They move to expand their existing space, to enhance their image or to improve upon their current location. First-time office users could be starting up a new business or moving out of a home-based office.

Regardless of the reason, moving offices is a major undertaking that can be time consuming and stressful. *Office Relocation Planner* can help by providing information unique to each phase of your move, along with detailed checklists and timelines.

Selecting Your Moving Team

Once the decision to move has been made, ensure your success by gathering and focusing company resources, including employees and professional consultants, to plan and manage the relocation.

The first step is to select an internal relocation team, including a project manager. Your project manager should be flexible and calm in a crisis and have enough authority that employees will respect his or her decisions. He or she will also need to be comfortable working with contractors, space planners, architects and all of your moving-related vendors. This role is typically given to the office manager or human resources director, although larger firms may have a facility manager that can be a natural choice to manage the relocation.

The relocation team should include a representative from each department in the company. Input from all areas and departments will make sure that fewer details are overlooked.

Keep the following in mind when choosing your team members:

- Select employees, preferably managers, who are organized and competent, communicate well, and have the ability to make good decisions.

- Those who accept the additional responsibility of being on the relocation team should understand that occasional evening and weekend work may be necessary.

- Make sure members of the relocation team are given the authority to make decisions on their department's behalf.

Members of the relocation team should be available for weekly progress meetings, as well as having the flexibility to complete their assigned relocation team tasks in addition to their existing workload.

If your company is very small, instead of a team, you may find that an individual employee can handle the moving process on his or her own.

Establish a Timeline

A typical move takes anywhere from six months to a year or more of planning. Lease negotiation delays, office design, permitting and construction setbacks are just some of the reasons why it is important to begin your search for office space early. The biggest risk in waiting too long to start your search is that you end up limiting your options.

Establish your ideal moving date, considering your current lease expiration or early termination date, if applicable. If your business is seasonal, be sure this date is planned for a non-peak time. Using the timeframes shown in the chart below, back up from your desired moving date to determine when you need to start the relocation process.

Average Relocation Timeframes

Space Size in SF	Timing
Up to 1,500	6-9 Months
1,500 - 4,000	9-12 Months
4,000 - 10,000	12-14 Months
10,000 – 25,000	14-18 Months
25,000 – 100,000+	18-24 Months

Keep in mind, if you intend to have a facility custom built, or if you anticipate significant remodeling of an existing location, additional time may be required. Conversely, if your business is able to lease space on an as-is basis, it is possible to complete the leasing process in a shorter timeframe.

Most importantly, the less time you leave for your office search, the more you may find yourself compromising, so don't hesitate to start the process early.

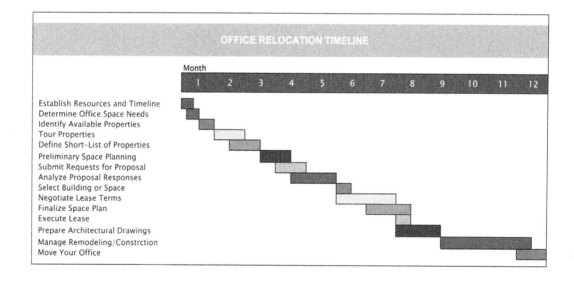

Determine Your Budget

Create a relocation budget, similar to the one shown on the following page, outlining the various costs that are associated with your relocation. Your budget should consider professional advisory fees, costs of hiring a moving company, relocating your equipment and computer network, replacing office furniture and printing new business cards, stationery and other materials. Moving expenses vary by region. If your company has moved in the past you may be able to estimate costs by checking your accounting files for receipts from the last relocation. If not, engage your advisory team to help determine budget values.

Relocation Budget

Monthly Facility Expenses

Rent and Other Monthly Expenses	Budget	Actual	Variance ($)	Variance (%)
Rent	$ 10,000	$ 11,500	$ 1,500	15.0%
Insurance	$ 1,200	$ 1,000	$ (200)	-16.7%
Communication/Networking Fees	$ 750	$ 800	$ 50	6.7%
Utilities	included in rent	$ -	$ -	0.0%
Common Area Maintenance	included in rent	$ -	$ -	0.0%
Property Taxes	included in rent	$ -	$ -	0.0%
Janitorial Services	included in rent	$ -	$ -	0.0%
Total Rent and Other Monthly Facility Expenses	$ 11,950	$ 13,300	$ 1,350	11.3%

Relocation Expenses

Location & Leasing Expenses	Budget	Actual	Variance ($)	Variance (%)
Attorney Fees	$ 2,500	$ 3,000	$ 500	20.0%
Architect/Space Planner	$ 5,000	$ 3,500	$ (1,500)	-30.0%
Communication/Network Consultant	$ 2,000	$ 2,200	$ 200	10.0%
Additional Tenant Improvements, not included in rent	$ 8,000	$ 10,500	$ 2,500	31.3%
Security Deposit	$ 10,000	$ 10,000	$ -	0.0%
Signage (may be included as negotiated lease term)	$ 2,500	$ 2,250	$ (250)	-10.0%
Network Cabling	$ 2,000	$ 2,125	$ 125	6.3%
Security System, door locks, alarms, etc.	$ 3,000	$ 2,750	$ (250)	-8.3%
Total Leasing & Location Expenses	$ 35,000	$ 36,325	$ 1,325	3.8%

Moving Expenses	Budget	Actual	Variance ($)	Variance (%)
Moving Vendor	$ 2,500	$ 2,700	$ 200	8.0%
Computer Relocation Vendor	$ 1,500	$ 1,800	$ 300	20.0%
Other Moving Vendors – Equipment/Artwork, etc.	$ 1,000	$ 700	$ (300)	-30.0%
Total Moving Expenses	$ 5,000	$ 5,200	$ 200	4.0%

New Equipment/Furnishings Expenses	Budget	Actual	Variance ($)	Variance (%)
Phone System	move existing	$ -	$ -	0.0%
Office Equipment, copiers, fax machines, etc.	lease	$ -	$ -	0.0%
Conferencing/Audio Visual Equipment	$ 2,000	$ 1,850	$ (150)	-7.5%
Computers	move existing	$ -	$ -	0.0%
Furnishings	$ 5,000	$ 5,200	$ 200	4.0%
Supplies	$ 1,500	$ 1,800	$ 300	20.0%
Breakroom/kitchen appliances	$ 500	$ 450	$ (50)	-10.0%
Total New Equipment/Furnishings Expenses	$ 9,000	$ 9,300	$ 300	3.3%

Printing/Marketing Expenses	Budget	Actual	Variance ($)	Variance (%)
Re-print stationery, business cards, etc.	$ 1,000	$ 1,200	$ 200	20.0%
Change website and online contact info, maps	$ 500	$ 450	$ (50)	-10.0%
Graphic designer fees, update ad slicks, etc.	$ 2,500	$ 1,975	$ (525)	-21.0%
Total Printing/Marketing Expenses	$ 4,000	$ 3,625	$ (375)	-9.4%

| **Total Relocation Expenses** | **$ 53,000** | **$ 54,450** | **$ 1,450** | **2.7%** |

Considerations

Planning and Coordinating Your Move

- *Evaluate the feasibility of renewing your current lease* before making the decision to relocate.

- *Consider discussing options with your landlord,* such as whether or not your company can expand or downsize if needed, at your current location.

- *Understand the termination clause in your current lease.* Determine whether you need to pay additional rent in the event of holdover or if you need to restore the premises to their condition prior to your tenancy of the space.

- *Make a list of all key lease dates,* including termination date of your lease and if written notice is required prior to vacating the premises.

- *Assembling a committee to coordinate the move* will help ensure every department's wants and needs are taken into account throughout the process.

- *Establish your approximate moving date well in advance* to ensure ample time for planning the relocation.

- *Consider both ongoing monthly rental expenses and one-time moving costs* when determining your relocation budget.

Action Steps

Planning and Coordinating Your Move

		Timing Prior to Move
		(in months)
☐	Appoint a relocation coordinator and/or relocation team.	12 – 14
☐	Schedule the prospective moving day, knowing that this may be a moving target until an office space is selected and other factors are determined.	12 – 14
☐	Determine your relocation budget including estimates for professional advisory fees, moving expenses, and the cost of new furnishings and equipment.	12 – 14

2 | Finding the Right Office Location

Any business relocation begins with a search for an appropriate facility. The facility search for smaller companies or start-up ventures is often relatively simple. For larger organizations the process can be more complicated and time-consuming. Whether your company has 10 employees or 10,000, determining the office space attributes for your business to run efficiently is a critical phase of the facility selection process.

Establish Your Office Space Criteria

There are numerous items to consider when identifying the criteria of your ideal office space, including your company's future plans, potential for growth, and employee and customer needs. Involve the relocation team and other employees in discussions about what works in your current space and what features are not very functional.

Some of the considerations that you should take into account for your new location include:

Cost of Occupancy

- Budgeted monthly or annual rental expense.
- Additional costs, e.g., utilities, real estate taxes, maintenance and janitorial services, if not included in the rental rate.

Location, Location, Location

- Downtown or suburban office park.
- Proximity to customers and employees.
- Ease of access, proximity to major roads and public transportation.
- Area amenities, restaurants, hotels, banking, etc.

Amount of Space Required

- Size of office space in square feet.
- Number of private offices, conference rooms and open spaces required.
- Is your business growing or shrinking?

Building Image

- What conclusions do you want your customers to draw from their perceptions of your building?
- Will the facility image enhance or detract from your ability to hire quality employees?

Where are the Employees?

- Do the majority of your employees live in a particular suburb or submarket?
- Will your company lose current employees as a result of relocating too far from where they live?
- Which locations will provide a sufficient employment base?
- Is availability of public transportation important?

Form and Function

- What type of space layout will best suit your organization – an open office with modular systems furniture or a more traditional environment with many private offices?
- Will your future needs require periodic changes in your work station configuration? If so, consider including more open areas in your proposed office space design. Open areas with modular furnishings can be reconfigured to

accommodate growth, providing flexibility within your space.

- Does the new facility allow for growth? Are there expansion opportunities within the building?

Parking

- What are your parking requirements for employees and visitors?
- Is covered parking required?

Other Factors to Consider

- Is building signage important to your business?
- Will your technology requirements be changing in the near future?
- Do you have a need for additional storage space for inventory or files?
- Do you require warehouse or production space?
- Consider additional space for servers, copiers, plotters and other office equipment.

Should You Hire a Commercial Real Estate Agent?

Many businesses hire consultants to handle various aspects of their relocation, the most common being a commercial real estate agent. In fact, commercial real estate agents are involved in the majority of commercial lease and purchase transactions. This is particularly the case in metropolitan areas, where a wide variety of properties are available.

Commercial agents are used on a regular basis because they add convenience and expertise to the facility selection process, saving the tenant or buyer, time and money. Their expertise and market knowledge can be invaluable in helping businesses examine and evaluate the facility alternatives available.

If you choose to select a commercial real estate broker, they will do much of the work described through the balance of this section. However, it is still important for you to remain in touch with the process. Your agent may have the market knowledge, but you are the expert on your business' needs. Remaining active in the process will ensure your organization's requirements are being considered and met.

How to Find Available Office Properties

Based upon the facility needs you have established, you are now ready to search for property which best meets these criteria. A commercial real estate agent is usually the best source for identifying available locations, but there are other resources. Commercial multiple listing services, such as Loopnet. com, offer public access; and many commercial listings are posted on various classified advertising websites.

One of the most basic methods of finding space is to visit your preferred geographic area looking for leasing signs that advertise office vacancies. While searching for properties, record the name and address of the building and the telephone number posted on the leasing sign. In some cases, instead of a sign in front of the building, there may be leasing information in the building lobby or on the directory sign. These signs will typically include contact information for the building's leasing agent or property manager where you can request further details.

The Perfect Property Tour

Once a list of possible property alternatives has been developed, schedule a time with the landlord or listing agent, to visit these properties in person. When touring the buildings, ask specific questions that will give insight to how the building meets your criteria. Information gathered from this tour will be used to eliminate many of the initial alternatives. It is suggested that as many buildings be visited on the same day as possible, allowing you to better compare the merits and nuances of each property while they are fresh in your mind.

The business decision maker and relocation team members should be present for the property tour. Depending on drive time between buildings, a tour of a single location typically takes from 30 to 60 minutes.

Other tools that can help identify each property's features are floorplans, flyers/brochures and building specification sheets. During the property tour, keep track of unanswered questions or missing floor plans that you would like to follow up on later.

Narrow the Alternatives

Based on the information gathered during the property tour, narrow the alternatives to the two or three properties that best suit your needs. This will be a manageable number of buildings from which to complete a more in-depth and detailed evaluation.

Space Planning

When you have determined your top two or three choices, it is time for an architect to provide a preliminary space plan to see how each of these options can be configured to best suit your needs.

How your business will fit in a particular space and what changes will be required is important because a landlord's economic terms will be dependent on the extent of construction and upgrades that your business will require.

An architect should create a preliminary space plan for each of the proposed spaces. These preliminary space plans are called a "test-fit." The expense of preliminary space planning is typically paid for by the landlord; it is part of his or her cost of doing business. Landlords either employ in-house designers, or they outsource their space planning needs. You can also bring in your own architect to design the preliminary plan, if you prefer.

Although several buildings may have spaces that appear to be similarly suitable for your business, once the test-fits are completed, the differences in function and efficiency may be significant.

Developing your Request for Proposal (RFP)

Once you have narrowed your search to two or three buildings and completed preliminary space planning, prepare a Request for Proposal (RFP) for each location (see example on page 18). The RFP process creates competition among landlords for your business.

Your RFP should request details on the following:

- Building Location
- Size of Space

- Lease Commencement Date
- Lease Term
- Rental Rate
- Security Deposit
- Tenant Improvement Allowance
- Option to Renew
- Expansion Option
- Signage
- Access
- Mechanical Systems
- Fire/Life Safety Systems
- Building Security
- Elevators
- Parking
- Building Ownership
- Property Management
- Building Amenities

Example Request for Proposal

Tenant Information:	The Easton Group, a Washington Corporation
Location/Address:	Presidio Center 3180 Creekside Dr., Suite 210
Size of Space:	6,827 square feet
Lease Commencement Date:	January 1
Lease Term:	Five (5) years
Rental Rate:	Propose the most aggressive rental rate possible. State any rent escalations during the lease term and any additional operating expenses that are not included in the rental rate.
Security Deposit:	Is a security deposit required for the space? If so, state the amount and terms of the deposit.

Tenant Improvement Allowance: What is the tenant improvement allowance for improvements to the proposed suite?

Option to Renew: Tenant requests one (1) option to renew the lease upon expiration, upon the same terms and conditions as the original lease, with the exception of rent, which will be at the market rate for space in the building, to be agreed upon by both tenant and landlord. Tenant will give landlord 120 days written notice of the tenant's intent to renew this lease.

Expansion Option: Describe how any potential need for expansion space can be met in this building. Tenant requests a Right of First Refusal on any adjoining space to Suite 210 that becomes available during the lease term.

Signage: What tenant signage will be provided at the landlord's expense? Are there additional signage opportunities available at the tenant's expense?

Access: Tenant requires 24-hour access to the leased premises.

Mechanical Systems: Describe the building's heating, ventilation and cooling (HVAC) system, including square feet per zone, hours of service, and whether there is a charge for after-hours usage.

Fire/Safety Systems: Describe the building's fire protection and safety systems.

Building Security: Does the landlord provide security in and around the building? What restrictions, if any, does the landlord have on tenants installing their own security system on the leased premises?

Elevators: How many elevators does the building have? Include information on both freight and passenger elevators.

Parking: Provide information on the parking ratio for the building and how it will accommodate the tenant's requirement for forty-two parking spaces (37 employee and 5 visitor spaces). Describe any additional costs associated with parking.

Building Ownership: Give an overview of the building ownership.

Property Management: What property management company is responsible for maintaining the building and are they located on site?

Building Amenities: Describe amenities available to tenants of the building.

Standard Lease: Please include a copy of your standard lease for the proposed building.

Submittal Information: Please submit your response within 10 business days.

In order to make an "apples-to-apples" comparison of the remaining alternatives, make certain the information contained in the Request for Proposal, which you will send to each landlord or agent, is consistent. Set a timeframe for the landlords who were solicited for a proposal to respond. Once you have received all proposals, prepare an analysis in spreadsheet form, example below, to compare how each of the alternatives stack-up. Whenever a landlord's response is unclear, contact the landlord or their agent and request further clarification.

Proposal Analysis

	Presidio Center	Corporate Center	1st Bank Plaza	City Center	USA Building
Address	3180 Creekside	1209 N. Capital	100 Central Park	245 E. 5th Ave.	100 USA Pkwy.
Area	6,287 SF	6,430 SF	6,175 SF	6,632 SF	6,440 SF
Lease Commencement	January 1	February 1	January 1	January 1	January 15
Lease Term	5 Years	7 Years	5 Years	5 Years	5 Years
Rental Rate	$21.75	$19.00	$23.00	$19.75	$20.50
Operating Expenses	Full Service	Net of utilities and janitorial	Full Service	Full Service	Net of utilities and janitorial
Security Deposit	One month rent	One month rent	Two months rent	Two months rent	One month rent
Tenant Improvement Allowance	$20.00/SF	$12.00/SF	$20.00/SF	$0.00/SF	$8.00/SF

Proposal Analysis, cont.

	Presidio Center	Corporate Center	1st Bank Plaza	City Center	USA Building
Option to Renew	(1) 5-year option at market rent	(1) 7-year option at market rent	Not available	(1) 5-year option at $23.75/ SF	(1) 5-year option at market rent
Expansion Option	Available	Available	Available	None available	Available
Signage	Lobby, suite entry	Monument, lobby, suite entry	Monument, suite entry	Lobby, suite entry	Monument, suite entry
Access	24 hr. access w/ key fob	24 hr. access w/ key card	24 hr. access w/tenant key	24 hr. access w/key fob	24 hr. access w/ key card
Mechanical Systems	Heat Pump system	Variable Air Volume system	Variable Air Volume system	Electrical split system	Heat Pump system
Fire/Safety Systems	Sprinklered/ Meets code	Sprinklered/ Meets code	Sprinklered/ Meets code	Sprinklered/ Meets code	Sprinklered/ Meets code
Building Security	Video monitor	Video monitor	On-site security guard	Video monitor	On-site security guard
Elevators	3 passenger/1 freight	4 passenger/1 freight	2 passenger/0 freight	6 passenger/1 freight	2 passenger/0 freight
Parking	4 spaces/ 1000sf	Off Site parking	4 spaces / 1000sf	3 spaces / 1000sf	Off Site parking
Building Ownership	Pension Fund	REIT	LLC	Partnership	Pension Fund
Property Mgmt. Co.	ABC Management	Building Mgmt. Co.	Wilson Mgmt.	ABC Management	Capitol Management
Building Amenities	Near restaurants, hotel	Bank, coffee shop in building	Cafeteria in building	Near restaurants, shopping	Fitness center in building

Selecting the Most Suitable Property

Once all clarifications have been received and the analysis is complete, the property, which will best suit the needs of your business, should be evident. If the decision is still unclear, schedule a time with the landlord or agent to visit each of the buildings again. This last visit may uncover further considerations in narrowing your choices for a facility.

Lease Review & Execution

After selecting the property that will best suit your business' needs, request that the landlord prepare a lease agreement. It is important for you to review the document carefully and to have an understanding of all of the terms and conditions of the lease agreement. Be sure that the lease includes all of the terms negotiated in the proposal. Because of the importance of this document, most businesses have their lease agreements reviewed by an attorney.

Signing the Lease

When the lease language has been finalized, the document is ready to be executed. Multiple copies of the lease and all exhibits, usually three or four, will be printed by the tenant, or delivered to the tenant for signature. More than one copy of the lease is signed by all parties so that each can retain a document with original signatures. The landlord, the tenant, and any brokerage firms involved in the transaction should each receive a fully executed original lease agreement.

The tenant is typically asked to sign the lease documents first. Documents signed by the tenant are then delivered to the landlord for signature. Plan to submit a check for any required deposits and first and/or last month's rent along with the signed documents.

Depending on the landlord's availability, it can take several days or longer before the lease is fully executed. It is important to note that the lease is not valid until it has been signed by both parties and the tenant should not consider the transaction complete until they are given an original lease document with all signatures.

Notifying Employees

If you haven't done so already, now is the appropriate time to notify your staff and employees of the upcoming move. Prepare a letter or email, similar to the one on the next page and send to all staff members as soon as a lease has been signed and plans are underway for the move.

Timing of employee notification of the move is important. Once the lease is signed, word of your plans will get out quickly among the real estate brokerage community and other vendors that may begin vying for your moving needs. You want to be able to control the announcement of your relocation plans. It is also important that the notification doesn't go out before the lease is signed. Lease negotiations occasionally fail, even up to the last moment before the lease is signed. It can cause unnecessary stress to announce a new location only to have it fall through.

Employee Notification Memo/Email Example

To: All Employees of The Easton Group

From: Taylor Jacobs

Subject: Office Relocation

I am very pleased to announce the relocation of our company to a new facility. As a result of The Easton Group's growth and change in office space requirements, we will be relocating our offices to 3180 Creekside Boulevard in the Creekside Business Park.

Our move is scheduled to occur over the weekend beginning at 5:00 p.m. on Friday, November 6th and we plan to be fully relocated to our new offices by 8:00 a.m. on Monday, November 9th. Further instructions on planning for the move will be sent out in the upcoming weeks.

In making this decision, many aspects of our business have been considered, most importantly of which is our employees. Although some of you may have a longer commute, I believe this move will benefit all of us through continued growth and the success of The Easton Group.

I look forward to working with all of you in making this move to our new space.

Sincerely,

Taylor Jacobs
Director

Considerations

Finding the Right Office Location

- *Interview several commercial real estate brokers.* Be sure to check references of the individual agents, as well as the companies they represent.

- *If in doubt as to the amount of space your business needs, plan for approximately 200 to 225 square* feet per person. If your space is more than 50% private offices, you may need a little extra space; if it is more than 50% open area, you could possibly use less.

- *Consider whether a specific building image* is critical to the success of your business. Certain types of businesses, such as attorneys and financial advisors, prefer to be in a more prestigious building or location.

- *Be sure to consider parking and transportation* for your employees and customers. If you are located in a congested area or you have minimal parking available, customers will be less likely to visit your office and you may also have trouble retaining employees.

- *When touring buildings, plan to see as many as possible on the same day.* If your tour will take more than one day, try to schedule your building tours on consecutive days.

- *Keep a file of any information you receive* from the landlord or agent, and take notes.

- *The space planner responsible for your office layout should verify the measurements* and requirements of both new and existing office furniture and workstations to insure a proper fit in the new office. Make the space planner aware of any oversized items you may have.

- ***Remember to include specific lease terms*** that are critical to your business, such as an option to renew or on-building signage, in the RFP.

- ***Determine insurance needs.*** Most landlords require personal property and general liability insurance of specific limits. The required coverage must be in effect, and you will need a "Certificate of Insurance" from your agent prior to your occupancy. Advise your insurance agent that the building owner must be named as an additional insured on the insurance policy.

- ***If you have extensive file or storage needs,*** find out if there is any unoccubiable space in the building that could be rented at a lower rate for storage, i.e. basement space, etc.

- ***Examine the lease for sign restrictions*** and approvals. Most landlords will require a drawing and specifications provided by the sign contractor, for sign approval.

- ***Invest in an experienced real estate attorney*** to review the terms of the lease to ensure that your company's interests are protected.

Action Steps

Finding the Right Office Location

		Timing Prior to Move
		(in months)
☐	Review what works and what doesn't work in your current space with your relocation and advisory teams.	11 – 12
☐	Interview and select a commercial real estate agent.	11 – 12
☐	Calculate the amount of square footage your business requires.	11 – 12
☐	With your commercial real estate agent's help, if using, develop your facility/site criteria, including all requirements that need to be met in your new location.	11 – 12
☐	Your commercial real estate agent, if using, will identify properties in your market which best meet your requirements and provide you with a property availability report.	10 – 12
☐	Contact landlords/real estate agents to set up appointments for property tours. (If you are using a broker, he or she will do this for you.)	10 – 12
☐	Tour selected buildings, take detailed notes.	9 – 11
☐	Narrow alternatives to a short list of two or three choices.	9 – 11
☐	Have an architect/space planner create test-fit floor plans for short-listed properties.	9 – 11
☐	Review test-fit floor plans, provide feedback to architect/space planner.	9 – 11
☐	Develop a Request for Proposal (RFP) based on your needs.	8 – 10
☐	Deliver the RFP to the landlords of the top two or three buildings you have chosen to pursue.	8 – 10

		Timing Prior to Move
		(in months)
☐	Receive RFP responses from landlords. Review RFP responses.	8 – 10
☐	Select most suitable property for your business, request lease from landlord.	6 – 8
☐	Have a decision-maker from your company, your commercial real estate agent, if using, and your real estate attorney review the lease.	6 – 8
☐	Ensure any negotiated lease revisions have been incorporated into the final lease document.	6 – 8
☐	Finalize space plan and interior color selections, construction should begin on space as soon as lease has been signed and final space plan has been approved.	6 – 8
☐	Request final lease documents, sign lease.	5 – 7
☐	Prepare and send employee notification memo/email to all staff members and employees of your company.	5 – 7

3 | Preparing for the Move

Now that the lease is signed, it's time to begin working on the logistics of your physical move. Start by determining your requirements for the move and outlining the scope of work.

Creating Your Office Moving Plan

Prepare an office moving plan and inventory list using the example on page 30. Once completed, this information will be the basis upon which you will compare the services offered by various moving vendors.

Your plan should include the following details:

- Target moving date

- Building address and suite number of current and new locations

- Furnishings and equipment to be moved

- Quantity estimates for moving and packing supplies

- License and insurance requirements for moving vendors

A clear plan will help you consistently convey what you will require from each moving vendor, making sure that none of the companies bidding for your job will omit important details. This will allow for a fair comparison of the bids you receive from each prospective moving vendor.

Office Moving Plan

Company and Location Information

Company Name:		Target Moving Date:	May 1
	Current Location	New Location	
Building Address			
Suite Number			
City, State ZIP			
Size (square feet)			
Special Instructions/ Building or Location Challenges			
	Company Contact	Moving Company Contact	
Contact			
Contact Phone			
Contact Email			

Inventory List

Item	Description	Quantity	Notes
Desks	Executive and task desks		
Credenzas	Secondary desk/worksurface		
Bookshelves	Book or storage		
Cubicles	Systems furniture		
Task Chairs	Chairs on wheels or rollers		
Conference Tables	Large or small		
Conference Chairs	Fixed chairs, arm or side		
Filing Cabinets	2-drawer and 4-drawer		
Desktop Computers	Desktop or tower		
Monitors	Computer monitors and TV's		
Copiers/Printers/Faxes	Multi-function machines, plotters		
A/V Equipment	Projection equipment, screens		
Telephone Handsets	Telephone equipment, handsets and headsets		
Other Equipment	Postage meters, plotters, scanners, etc.		
Office Supplies	General quantities of supplies		

Moving Supplies

Supply Type	Description	Quantity	Notes
File Boxes	10" x 12" x 15" or similar		
Small Boxes	12" x 12" x 16" or similar		
Medium Boxes	18" x 18" x 16" or similar		
Large Boxes	18" x 18" x 24" or similar		
Wardrobe Boxes	24" x 24" x 40" or similar		
Tape	2" wide, 2.2 millimeter		
Tape Dispensers	Hand-held		
Packing Materials	Bubble-wrap, paper		
Markers	Heavy-duty, black		

Vendor Requirements

Requirement	Description	Yes/No	Notes
License	Must be licensed in applicable state(s)		
Insurance	Must carry appropriate insurance for loss and damage		
Equipment	Confirm vendor has appropriate equipment for the job		

Target Moving Date

Start by establishing your target moving date. Move-in dates usually co-incide with completion of the Tenant Improvements and delivery of the Certificate of Occupancy. However, in some cases, tenants are able to move furnishings and equipment into the space before construction is fully completed.

Work with the landlord or property manager to determine the timeframe when your space will be move-in ready. Then, choose a target date within the timeframe that works for your business. Many companies schedule the move on a Friday and give employees the option to come in over the weekend and unpack. It may be possible to schedule the move for a Saturday, although there could be an added charge for weekend service.

Location Information

Clearly identify your current location and future location including suite numbers, if applicable. State the size of each space in square feet; this will give your moving vendors a feel for the scope of work. If you know of any challenges or special instructions for either location, be sure to include this information on your plan. Special instruction will include information on scheduling a freight elevator or moving van parking restrictions.

Furniture and Equipment Assessment

The moving plan should include an assessment of all items that will be relocated to the new space. List furniture, cubicles, chairs, computers, equipment and supplies that will be moved. In addition, determine if any new furniture and equipment are needed. The following chapters provide information on ordering and lead times for these items. Make a note of any over-sized or unique equipment that may require specialized packing or moving services.

Packing and Unpacking

Determine whether you prefer employees or the moving company to pack and unpack files, desk contents and office supplies. Employees typically pack and unpack their own work areas, but moving companies can also provide this service. Balance the cost of professional packing/unpacking against employee workload. You may find that it is worth the expense of professional packing services to maintain employee productivity during the move.

Moving Supplies

Next, request vendors provide information on the quantity and type of boxes and moving supplies needed, and have them include a quote for these items. Each moving company you consider may handle boxes and supplies differently. Some will directly charge for supplies and include the charge as a line item in their proposal; others may offer to include boxes free of charge. Either way there is a cost of the supplies that your company will end up paying for.

Consider asking for proposals with and without supplies to determine what you will be charged for these materials. Many office supply stores and on-line retailers sell moving supplies at discounted pricing and some offer free delivery.

If desired, assess the overall costs of moving company supplied materials versus purchasing them from another source. The decision on your source for moving supplies can be made closer to your moving date. Keep in mind that if the selected moving company will be packing and unpacking, the mover will likely require supplying their own boxes and materials.

License and Insurance Requirements

Verify that you will only deal with licensed and insured vendors by including your requirements for these items on your moving plan. If a specific level of insurance is needed, make sure your plan clearly states this information.

Staging the Move

Businesses with less than 100 employees can usually relocate their furnishings, equipment and supplies within a one to two day period. Larger firms will want to schedule the move in stages. A staged move is best accomplished by scheduling separate department moves. Determine optimal relocation timing for each department and set the moving schedule accordingly.

Consider interaction between departments and whether it may be critical to not have two or more specific departments relocating at the same time. For instance, if having the sales and marketing departments unproductive on the same day will hurt your sales, schedule these groups for different moving dates. Indicate whether your relocation will occur in stages on your moving plan.

Considerations

Preparing for the Move

- ***Establish your target moving date as soon as the lease is signed.*** Schedule the move on an appropriate date near the completion and delivery of your new space.

- ***Ask the property manager or landlord at both your current and new locations if there are any restrictions placed on the time of day, or day of week you move.*** Many landlords require moves to take place after normal business hours or on weekends and this information will need to be included on your moving plan.

- ***Determine whether the mover or your employees will be packing.*** Most movers recommend that individuals pack their own desks and personal items.

- ***Create a moving plan with details of both locations and a list of all items to be moved;*** distribute your plan to all prospective moving vendors to ensure that each of their quotes are based on the same information.

- ***If you anticipate the move taking more than one day***, consider dividing your move into multiple stages.

Action Steps

Preparing for the Move

		Timing Prior to Move
		(in days)
☐	Contact property managers at current and new locations to determine any restrictions on timing of your move. (Time of day restrictions, specific exits/elevators, etc.)	180
☐	Determine target moving date.	180
☐	Inventory furniture and equipment. Identify which items will be moved.	180
☐	Create moving plan with detailed inventory list, location and scheduling information.	180

4 | Selecting an Office Moving Company

Choosing a moving company is one of the most obvious yet underrated aspects of the relocation process. Don't expect the company who moved you into your home will be equally qualified to perform a commercial move. Moving companies with little experience in office relocations may have difficulty delivering the service needed for a smooth transition into your new facility.

The more experienced the mover, the less time you will need to spend managing their crew during the actual move. Depending on the size of the relocation, many moving companies will have a supervisor on site coordinating their employees' efforts. This frees you to focus on other issues that come up on moving day.

Begin your search for a commercial mover early, at least three to six months ahead of your anticipated move date. Consider that it may take several weeks to prepare a moving plan, interview candidates, receive and review bids and select a vendor.

Interviewing Moving Companies

Plan on interviewing and getting quotes from at least three moving companies. Schedule an interview meeting with each prospective vendor at your existing office so they can see the items to be moved and understand any constraints of the building and location. Provide each moving company with a copy of your moving plan.

If you don't know of a good commercial mover in your area, ask for a referral. Your commercial real estate agent should know of several qualified movers, and so should other tenants in your current or new building. Your local Better Business Bureau or Chamber of Commerce can also help with a moving company referral.

When interviewing moving companies, be sure you understand all of the rates and charges that may apply. You will also want to determine whether they are available on your preferred pickup and delivery dates and times. Be aware that there may be additional charges for after-hours or weekend moves.

Verify that each moving company you interview is able to handle the relocation of computers and other technology devices. Confirm they have the experience and required equipment (computer carts and anti-static protective bags or wrap) to move these items.

Make sure the moving companies you are considering are equipped to handle your unique needs. For example, there are commercial movers who specialize in moving inventory or heavy equipment usually found in warehouses or industrial facilities. If you have a high-density office configuration that utilizes workstations, choose a mover with experience in moving panel systems.

Licensing and Insurance

Request proof of proper licensing and insurance from each moving company. It is also important to understand what liability they have for both the condition of your current and new location, as well as for your furnishings and equipment. Each company you interview should be able to provide detailed answers to the following questions.

- What are the limits for liability coverage, property loss and damage?

- How is the value of the office contents established?

- What is the maximum dollar amount of insurance provided by the moving company?

- What is the procedure for filing a claim?

- How quickly are claims processed?

The amount of insurance offered by most moving companies typically does not cover the full replacement value of your belongings and supplemental insurance may be required. Check with your own insurance agent to determine if you need additional coverage.

Checking Moving Company References

Ask each moving company to provide references, along with contact information. Call each of the references and ask the following questions:

- When did your move occur? (Determines if you are speaking with a recent customer.)

- Were you satisfied with the performance of the moving company?

- Did the movers arrive on schedule and complete the job in a timely manner?

- Did the movers treat your furnishings and equipment with care?

- Was there any damage to your furnishings and equipment?

- Was there any damage to either your old or new location?

- Were any damage claims made? If so, was the claim handled to your satisfaction?

- How close was the moving company's final bill to their original estimate?

- Would you use this particular moving company again?

Get a Proposal

Request a written proposal from each moving company, instructing them to address all details in your moving plan.

As you review the proposals, remember that the proposal quotes are estimates and some moving companies may underestimate in order to win your business. If one of the proposals comes in considerably lower than the others, double-check to make sure the requirements of your move were fully understood and that the estimate is accurate. References will likely inform you of a moving company that consistently underbids in order to win business, and then bills their clients for a higher amount when the job is completed.

Considerations

Selecting an Office Moving Company

- *Share consistent information* with all potential moving companies in order to get comparable bids.

- *Remember that bids are only estimates* and some moving companies may underestimate in order to win your business. Always confirm their accuracy by comparing each of the proposals for the amount of man-hours the mover estimates.

- *Check references that are current*, because many moving companies experience rapid turnover in employees. Ask if the movers were cooperative and careful, and how closely they kept to their estimate.

- *Make sure your moving company is equipped to handle your unique needs.* For example, there are industrial movers who specialize in moving inventory or heavy equipment usually found in warehouses or industrial facilities.

- *Discuss the relocation of your computers and server equipment with your IT consultant.* If they are comfortable with having your moving company relocate the equipment, make certain your mover has the experience and necessary equipment for such a move.

- *Determine if the mover will supply boxes* and packing materials.

- *Request detailed information on insurance coverage and the claims procedure.* Make sure the moving company will repair any damage to the premises incurred by their employees.

- ***Choose and schedule the moving company early.*** Most leases terminate at the end of the month, making this a natural activity peak for commercial movers.

- ***Enlist your mover's expertise*** to offer solutions and to identify ways of saving money on your move.

Action Steps

Selecting an Office Moving Company

		Timing Prior to Move
		(in days)
☐	Schedule three movers to perform a site visit of your current location and to prepare estimates based on your moving plan and inventory list.	150
☐	Review moving company estimates, verify each company meets licensing and insurance requirements.	120
☐	Contact references provided by each moving company.	100
☐	Select moving company, schedule moving date.	100

5 | Connecting Your Office Space

Information technology (IT) and telecommunications is changing rapidly, more so than any other component related to your office space and a successful relocation. A smooth transition of your computer network and phone system between facilities will ensure continuity and prevent any data loss, as well as minimize your company's downtime.

Many businesses will use their relocation as an opportunity to upgrade or replace their computer equipment and phone system with new technology. In these cases, the existing equipment can be operated up to the day of the relocation. The new system and equipment can be installed prior to moving day and be fully operational immediately.

If new furniture is ordered, schedule it to be installed first and then have the technology equipment delivered and set up at each workstation or desk location. If existing furniture is being relocated, it may be easier to move this equipment after your existing furnishings are delivered to the space, typically the day of or the day after the move.

Alternatively, some companies choose to relocate their existing equipment from their current space to the new facility. In this case, you will need to identify the best time to make the transition from one office to the next, ideally during a weekend or overnight in order to maximize productivity during working hours.

Enlist Your IT Consultant

The importance of IT coupled with the fact that it is constantly changing highlight the need to have an IT consultant providing the most current advice available for your move.

Whether you have an IT specialist in-house or contract with an outside consultant, bring this person into the process early and keep them involved in the design of your space and network system needs. Your IT consultant will advise on the network cabling of your space and may also have input on design, construction and furnishings.

Planning Your Network

Your IT consultant will work closely with you to develop a comprehensive plan for your network, voice and cabling needs. This process should include the following steps:

- Establish technology requirements for the new facility.

- Assess your current equipment and software.

- Determine whether any additional equipment or software are required and assist with developing a budget if adding or upgrading is necessary.

- Compare cost of relocating equipment vs. replacing, consider technological advancements that may enhance productivity.

- Analyze potential carriers for internet and voice service.

- Develop a backup and testing plan to ensure all systems are operational after the move.

- Create disposition plan for any excess equipment and ensure all company data is wiped clean prior to disposition.

Make sure you plan adequately for your current and future cabling requirements. It is significantly easier and less expensive to have an adequate amount of cable, and to have ample voice and data outlets installed before you move, than to make changes afterward.

Network/Voice Cabling and Electrical

Your cabling strategy will need to consider voice and data. Some devices can use the less expensive Category 3 cable, however, your network connections should use higher-quality Category 5 cable in the jacks and patch panels. Plenum-rated cable may be required to comply with fire-code regulations. (In office space construction, the plenum is the space between the structural ceiling and the suspended ceiling that is used for air circulation in heating and air conditioning systems.)

Network/voice cabling and electrical outlets need to be placed appropriately on office walls and in workstation panels. If your future location requires a significant remodel or a new build-out, the space planner or architect will include the cabling and electrical outlets on your final space plan. The quantity and location of these outlets will be confirmed during the space planning process. When a space is being taken in close to as-is condition, verify that the existing outlet locations are adequate and if not, be sure to request additional connections as needed.

The following example shows a workstation with the typical locations of electrical and network/voice cabling outlets specified.

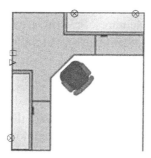

⊗	Double Electrical Outlet
∇	Voice Cable Outlet
☐	Double Electrical Outlet

Workstation Outlet Configuration

Private offices should be configured in a similar fashion. Consider including two data/voice cabling outlets on each wall of private offices and conference rooms to allow for future changes to the furniture layout.

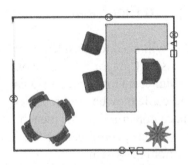

⊗   Double Electrical Outlet

∇   Voice Cable Outlet

☐   Double Electrical Outlet

Private Office Outlet Configuration

Evaluating Your Phone System

Carefully consider whether your current phone system is adequate for your needs or if it needs to be expanded, upgraded or replaced. If you determine an expansion or replacement system is required, a move is a good time to upgrade features.

In addition to the core set of features that any business requires, such as voicemail, call forwarding and conferencing, consider enhancing your system with advanced features. Several advanced features are now available and are providing significant benefits to more and more companies. These include:

- Location services that allow distributed workgroups in multiple locations to operate on a single phone system, especially important if you have employees that work remotely.

- Computer Telephony Integration (CTI) offers the ability to make calls from a computer by clicking on a contact's phone number. CTI can be an important feature for companies that use a customer relationship management (CRM) application.

- Intelligent call routing (Find me/Follow me) automatically forwards calls to employees' mobile phones or other designated phone numbers.

Consider your future communication needs, to the extent possible, and build at least five years of growth capacity into the new phone system.

The entire process of choosing and purchasing a new phone system can take 60 to 90 days.

If your telecommunications needs exceed 100 telephones, you should add lead-time to this estimate; consult with the vendors regarding their required lead-time for system delivery and place your order in a timely manner.

Keeping Your Phone Numbers

It is obvious that keeping your current telephone numbers is ideal both for simplicity and marketing. Consider the ability to transfer your existing numbers when evaluating potential office locations. Contact your local telephone company to determine your options for taking your current numbers to another location.

If it is not possible to keep your current phone number, call forwarding to your new number may be available. Call forwarding is normally offered at no charge for a set period of time, which will vary depending on your local service provider. You may be able to extend this period by paying a fee.

Toll-free numbers should be transferable to your new location as well. Contact your long distance/toll-free service provider as soon as possible to make them aware of your move and to find out if there are any changes that will need to be made to your service.

Some landlords offer a shared telecommunications service. This is a pooling of the phone usage of tenants in the building or office complex in order to get volume discounts, some of which are then passed on to the tenants. This is often a less expensive option. Check with your new landlord to see if shared telecommunications service is available.

Back Up Your Data

An important aspect of relocating a network is to create a backup of your company's computer and network data, ideally stored at an off-site location during the move in case your network is accidentally damaged.

Consider developing a disaster plan, in the event of a worst-case scenario. Although it is unlikely the plan will ever be used, if it is needed, having one could mean the difference between a minimal loss of productivity and partial to complete loss of data.

Considerations

Connecting Your Office Space

- *Involve your IT consultant* in the move from the beginning of the process. Whether this person is in-house or an outside consultant, they can help prevent your company from making costly errors, which occur frequently when information technology issues are overlooked.

- *Add as many voice and data outlets* as needed to accommodate future growth.

- *Determine if you will need wireless* connectivity, either in zones or your entire space.

- *Consider relocation of your company's network* at a time of low activity, i.e. overnight or on a weekend. This will give ample time to install and restore the system before it is placed back in service.

- *Make arrangements to have a dedicated power source installed* at your new location for your network server. Ask your equipment vendor if you are unsure about whether dedicated power is needed for particular items.

- *Check with your landlord to see if they offer shared telecommunications services* in your new facility.

- *Allow for 5 years' growth* potential when choosing and configuring a new phone system.

- *The location of the new facility may affect your ability to maintain your current phone number.* If keeping your current phone number is important, check with your local service provider to determine its geographic limitations.

- ***If not provided by the manufacturer, have your telephone system vendor prepare a "cheat sheet,"*** summarizing the basic operation of the telephones. Provide one to each employee with their phone at the new location.

- ***During the move, keep track of all server, network equipment and computer cables, power cords and phone wiring.*** Label cords accordingly and keep them with their specific piece of equipment. Something as simple as placing peripheral computer equipment (such as cables and the mouse) in a plastic bag and attaching it to the computer with packing tape will eliminate headaches later when reinstalling the system.

Action Steps

Connecting Your Office Space

	Timing Prior to Move (in days)
☐ Inventory existing computers, server and telecommunications equipment.	180
☐ Identify current telecommunication usage and future needs.	150
☐ Decide whether to relocate your existing server(s), computers and telephone system or if new equipment needs to be purchased.	150
☐ If a new telephone system, server equipment, or computers are required, make arrangements to interview vendors and begin the selection process.	150
☐ Review phone system and new equipment proposals, select vendors and order equipment.	120
☐ Establish the network and data cabling requirements at your new facility, with the assistance of your IT consultant.	120
☐ Select three voice and network cabling companies to review the space plan and tour the new facility to determine your cabling needs. Have each company submit a proposal for the services you'll require.	120
☐ Select three long distance providers to submit quotes for their services. (Remember to check with your new landlord on the availability of shared telecommunication services.)	90
☐ Choose voice and data cabling vendor. Schedule installation to occur 30 days before your move-in date. Coordinate with landlord and/or building contractor.	90
☐ Review long distance proposals, select provider and order long distance service.	75

	Timing Prior to Move
	(in days)
☐ Order or set up the transfer of phone and fax numbers.	75
☐ Contact all carriers and internet service providers (ISP's) with information on your new location and your anticipated move date.	75
☐ Make arrangements for phones to be operational on moving day. If necessary, have phones forwarded to temporary locations or cell phones during the actual move.	60
☐ Have cabling vendor begin installation at new facility.	30
☐ Confirm your network consultant is available to shut down your network immediately prior to your actual move and to restore the network at the new location as soon as feasible.	30
☐ Test all network and phone drops as soon as cabling vendor completes installation.	5
☐ Install new phone system at new location, if applicable.	5
☐ Assign employee phone numbers or extensions.	5
☐ Back up all company data. Require employees using personal computers to back up their own hard drives.	1
☐ Have your network consultant on hand near the end of the day immediately prior to your move to shut down the network. Make sure all employees have plenty of notice and are aware of the shutdown date and time.	1
☐ Restore and test the network as soon as computer equipment is installed at the new location.	0
☐ Review telephone system programming and routing, make any necessary changes.	-1

		Timing Prior to Move
		(in days)
☐	Hold training session for employees to learn new phone system, if applicable. Have phone system representative on hand to answer questions and assist with any issues that have come up.	-1 to -5
☐	Arrange to donate or recycle any network or telecommunications equipment that is no longer needed.	-7 to -30

6 | Moving Office Equipment

Office equipment is a broad category that includes machines other than computers, servers and telephones. Most offices have numerous types of equipment that fall under this category such as multi-function office machines, printers, copiers, plotters, scanners, fax machines, audio/visual conferencing equipment, projectors and postage meters.

Evaluate your equipment prior to moving to determine if any items are outdated or inefficient. Replacing older equipment can enhance productivity and may save money in the long run. For instance, newer equipment typically requires fewer service calls and replacement supplies (ink, toner, etc.) may be easier to find and less expensive.

Leased Equipment

Before moving any type of office equipment, verify whether your company owns or leases each item. Many businesses find that it makes more sense to lease copiers and printers while owning most of the other types of equipment. Office equipment vendors usually prefer to handle and move their own leased equipment or contract to have the items moved by a specialty office equipment mover. Equipment covered under a service contract is often leased, as well. Leased items will typically have a label, either on the top or on the side, which includes the leasing company's name and phone number.

Because of liability issues, movers should not relocate leased equipment unless you have the prior written approval of the equipment vendor. Check with your equipment vendors to verify their equipment relocation policy.

Office Equipment Preparation

In spite of their ability to stand up to frequent use and everyday wear and tear, copiers and printers are sensitive machines and should be handled with the utmost care.

Contact your copier and printer service vendors and ask for specific moving instructions, including any pre- and post-move servicing recommendations. At a minimum, ink and toner cartridges will typically need to be removed prior to relocation. Other equipment, such as inkjet printers, plotters, scanners, fax machines and postage meters, should be repackaged in their original cartons, if possible. If you don't have the original packaging materials, ask your mover to provide the appropriate boxes and packing material for these items.

Printers, scanners and other items connected to personal computers should be disconnected and packed individually. Whenever possible, remove power cords, place them in a plastic bag, and tape them to the top or back of each piece of equipment.

Security System

Most office buildings have some level of security; however, a security system specific to a particular space within a building is typically the tenant's responsibility. If you already own a system at your current space, check with your vendor to see if it can be relocated to the new facility. If so, schedule to have the security system removed from your existing location and reinstalled at your new office.

Beverage and Vending Machines

Coffee service, bottled water dispensers and vending machines should also be moved by the company that services each particular piece of equipment. Call your beverage and vending machine vendors to confirm that they can relocate these items.

Considerations

Moving Office Equipment

- *As a general rule, equipment that is leased must be handled and moved* by the equipment's vendor. Check with your equipment leasing company for their moving guidelines and requirements.

- *Determine if a dedicated power source* is needed at your new location for your copier/printer and any other equipment requiring dedicated electrical power.

- *Check with your insurance company* prior to moving to make certain all equipment is adequately covered under your existing policy during relocation.

- *During the move, keep track of all equipment cables, power cords and phone wiring.* Label cords accordingly and keep them with their specific piece of equipment.

- *Update or renew all service agreements,* licenses, equipment leases, etc. Negotiate more favorable terms whenever possible.

- *Keep all equipment manuals and service logs* in a centralized location during the move to keep them from being misplaced.

Action Steps

Moving Office Equipment

	Timing Prior to Move
	(in days)
☐ Determine whether any equipment needs to be upgraded or replaced.	150
☐ Make arrangements to interview office equipment vendors and begin the selection process, if new equipment is needed.	120
☐ Review office equipment vendor proposals, select equipment vendors.	120
☐ Place orders for new office equipment and set delivery on or before your move-in date.	90
☐ If existing copiers and/or printers will be moved, contact vendors to schedule removal of toner and determine whether they would prefer to move the equipment. If so, schedule moving date with vendors.	90
☐ Check with your security system vendor to determine if components at your current location can be relocated, if applicable.	60
☐ If you have bottled water, coffee service and/or vending machines, arrange for their respective vendors to relocate this equipment.	45
☐ Take delivery of copiers and printers at new location; verify that the toner has been replaced and that the equipment is operational. Make sure you have two extra toner cartridges on hand for each piece of equipment. Place order for additional supplies, if necessary.	0

		Timing Prior to Move
		(in days)
☐	Verify that coffee service equipment, water cooler and vending machines have been delivered and are operational. Ensure there are adequate levels of supplies for each (coffee, water bottles, disposable cups, etc.).	-1
☐	Arrange to donate or recycle obsolete equipment.	-7 to -30

7 | Relocating and Purchasing Office Furniture

You can enhance the image of your office and improve employee productivity by outfitting your new space with the right furnishings for the purpose. Most office plans include a combination of traditional furnishings and workstations. Even if you have existing furniture that you plan to move, you may need to order some additional pieces to fill in the gaps. Or, you may prefer to purchase entirely new furnishings for your future office. Regardless of which scenario you choose, there are special considerations to take into account and it is important to have a plan.

Evaluating Your Furniture Needs

Just as you analyzed your requirements for new office space, analyze the type of furniture and workstations that best meet your needs. By identifying your organizational or departmental needs, you can focus your future furniture purchases on one, or just a few models of a particular line. This will help to standardize the furnishings for each particular job and function. Ideally, all workstations in a department should be the same size and brand and have similar components. Standardizing your furniture provides flexibility of interchanging parts and layout and maintains a consistent, organized look to your office.

Systems Furniture

If your space plan includes open areas, you will likely require systems furniture. One advantage of systems furniture is that it can easily be installed and reconfigured, providing flexibility in the event you need to rearrange or add more units in the future.

Systems furniture has come a long way from the days of the ubiquitous gray cubicle. Manufacturers now provide a wide range of products including wired panels, desks and storage units that are designed to be used together in an open plan environment.

Workstation Components

Panels

The key component to systems furniture is the panels that make up the wall frames. Desktops, file cabinets and storage units are usually mounted directly to the wall panels. Ranging in height from 30 to 80 inches, panel height affects the amount of privacy in each cube.

Thirty-inch partitions allow for communication between desks and are often used for interactive jobs such as collaborative teams. Fifty-inch panels provide greater privacy for phone calls, but allow for conversation between stations when people are standing. The tallest panels afford enough privacy for intensive tasks or to hold meetings.

One of the most significant decisions you will make when purchasing systems furniture will be whether to buy wired or non-wired panels. Wired panels have electrical wiring in the framing of the panels, allowing for an adequate supply of electrical, networking and phone outlets to the desktop.

If you choose to install non-wired panels, you will need to make certain the new facility will provide enough electrical outlets to meet your needs. Obviously, wired furniture systems provide you with more flexibility. The only disadvantage of wired systems is the cost, which is generally 15 - 20% higher than non-wired systems.

Worksurfaces

Worksurfaces are constructed from a variety of different materials, including plastic and wood laminates. Generally, plastic laminate will be the less expensive option. For additional flexibility, many manufacturers now offer worksurfaces that allow adjustment from 25" to 49" in height so that employees can alternate between sitting and standing positions. Grommets, or openings, are built into worksurfaces to facilitate the management of power cords and telephone cables.

Workstation Storage

Storage above, below or next to the work surface is available. Open shelving and overhead bins offer convenient above-the-desk access without taking up valuable floor space. These options either hang from the panel wall or are placed on top of a worksurface.

Pedestal storage consists of regular and file drawer units placed under the worksurface. To increase mobility, pedestals can be purchased with wheels. Lateral files, bookshelves and credenzas can be included for additional storage.

Workstation Configurations

In order to determine which components your workstations will need, compile an inventory of what types of office and communications equipment each station will be required to support, including storage requirements and whether bookshelves will be necessary. Your architect or furniture consultant can then use this information to assist you in choosing the appropriate workstation components to suit your needs and location.

The following diagram shows common workstation configurations.

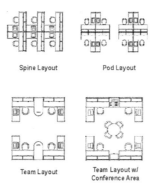

Spine Layout   Pod Layout

Team Layout   Team Layout w/ Conference Area

Workstation Configurations

Workstation Seating

When making decisions on the right chair for the job, consider how long the person will be sitting and what functions they will perform. Employees who sit most of the day should have high-tech chairs with ergonomic controls that let each user adjust the chair to suit his or her body size and work style.

Employees who spend most of the day sitting in front of a computer will need adjustable armrests to maintain a comfortable position at the keyboard. Their chairs should also have a tilt feature allowing users to look at the computer screen at a comfortable angle.

Workstation Installation

Relocation of systems furniture is more complicated than traditional office furniture. Any existing systems furniture you are planning to move will have to be disassembled prior to relocation, and then reassembled at the new office. Oftentimes moving companies are able to dismantle and move systems furniture, but some are not equipped to reassemble these items. Your furniture vendor will have more experience relocating your particular brand of furniture and may be a preferred option.

Furniture vendors either have their own installation crews, or have a relationship with a vendor who can perform this service. Contact your furniture vendor to determine if they can perform the disassembly, relocation and reassembly work, or if they can provide a referral for a workstation installation contractor. Make certain that the vendor you choose is competent and is familiar with your brand of system furniture.

Private Office Furniture

Private offices are typically furnished with case-goods: furnishings made of hard materials, such as wood, metal, glass or plastic. These items include desks, credenzas, file cabinets and bookshelves. Let your architect know what existing furniture you plan to move and if there are any gaps that need to be filled. He or she can then determine what is needed and include these items in the finished layout.

Executive Desks and Credenzas

Executive furnishings come in a number of different sizes and configurations; the most common is the pedestal design. Pedestal desks and credenzas feature a stacked drawer pedestal on both ends of the desk, which support a large desktop. There is an opening in the center, between the pedestals, for seating. Each pedestal usually contains a deep file drawer and one or two smaller drawers for pencils and other office supplies. Pedestal credenzas can either have an opening in the center for seating, similar to the desk; or there may be additional storage in the place of the opening.

Other variations of the pedestal desk include the L-shaped desk and U-shaped desk, which combine the desk and one or two credenzas to give the appearance of a single piece of furniture. Modern desks may have technology features, such as an under-mounted keyboard tray or a built-in power strip. Executive furnishings are commonly made from high-quality materials, including solid wood, metal and glass.

Coordinate the size of the furnishings with the room dimensions. Furniture that is too large or too small for the space will have an awkward look and will detract from the appearance of the office. When measuring an office for furnishings, be sure to take the door swing dimension into consideration.

Executive Seating

When choosing a chair for a private office make sure it fits with the desk, both in style and size. Executive desks are considerably less flexible in their size and shape than cubicles and the chair will need to fit precisely. Choosing an adjustable chair will help. Also, the style of the chair should blend with the rest of the office décor. Executives may not need all the performance features as they spend less time sitting down, however, chairs made of leather, wood or high-tech materials project a strong, professional image.

Reception Area

Configuring the reception area includes choosing between constructing a built-in front desk and purchasing a modular unit. The beauty of built-in furniture must be weighed against its permanence and inflexibility; while a modular unit can be added to or moved if your needs change.

Conference Rooms

Conference rooms are typically furnished with a table and chairs sized appropriately to the room, and often include additional cabinets for equipment storage. Modular sets of smaller tables that fit together to form a larger piece provide maximum flexibility. When selecting conference room chairs, consider the style of your office and the image you want to project. Also, determine the number of seats you will need at the table. If you need a few extra chairs around the table, choosing seating with a narrower profile may do the trick.

Breakroom

As with your conference room furniture, consider modular tables for the breakroom that can be configured in a variety of different ways. Any required appliances, such as a refrigerator, dishwasher and microwave, should be included in the space plan. Include water lines, if needed, for a coffee maker, refrigerator and ice machine.

Storage

Efficient storage is an important part of a wall-designed office. Lateral files, freestanding storage cabinets, bookshelves and built-in cabinets should be considered as part of your overall furnishings plan.

Ergonomics

Reducing ergonomic stress and injuries can increase employee productivity and reduce time off for illness or injury.

Neck aches, headaches, wrist aches and backaches are a few of the common risks of working in an office all day. These are real problems that can be addressed by offering good-quality and fully adjustable seating, desk tops that can be altered in height and correctly positioned monitors.

For additional help in this area consult a medical health professional who specializes in workspace ergonomic assessments.

Considerations

Relocating and Purchasing Office Furnishings

- ***Develop an in-house standard*** for your systems furniture. Consider the height, color scheme, brand and whether or not they need to be wired. This will allow for the flexibility to interchange components and rearrange the layout at any time.

- ***Determine your furniture and workstation needs early*** and place orders as soon as possible. Many furniture brands must be special-ordered and could have a 10- to 12-week lead time, if not longer.

- ***If ordering new furniture, request acknowledgments of all orders*** and shipping confirmations from the manufacturer. Have your furniture vendor confirm that the furniture will be delivered to your new facility prior to your move, with enough time for assembly. This is particularly important for systems furniture.

- ***Confirm that any large or oversized furnishings*** will fit in the new space. Take measurements of furniture and doorways, etc.

- ***If your workstations are wired, you will need additional co-ordination of telephone*** and network cabling. Wired systems also require adequate electrical service for connection to the workstations. Make sure this has been provided for in your space plan.

- ***Determine if desktop or workstation lighting*** will be needed, in addition to the overhead ceiling lights.

- ***Consider ergonomics when ordering furniture,*** workstations, and desk chairs in order to reduce computer-related injuries.

Action Steps

Relocating and Purchasing Office Furnishings

		Timing Prior to Move
		(in days)
☐	Determine whether any furnishings need to be replaced, upgraded or purchased.	210
☐	Select vendors to interview, evaluate product lines, and review budget requirements, if new furniture is required.	210
☐	Have each furniture vendor provide an office furniture layout and proposal.	180
☐	Review furniture proposals, check references and select a furniture vendor.	150
☐	Based on your furniture vendor's layout and proposal, determine your actual furnishing needs and place order with vendor.	150
☐	If moving any existing workstations, schedule your furniture vendor to disassemble at your old location and reassemble at your new location.	60
☐	Schedule delivery and assembly of new furniture, if applicable, preferably prior to moving day.	30
☐	Plan for disposal of furniture that will not be needed. Consider reselling or donating.	30
☐	Furniture vendor to dismantle existing workstations to be moved.	1
☐	Furniture vendor to re-assemble workstations in new location.	-1
☐	Verify that all systems furniture is assembled and configured per the vendor's proposal.	-2
☐	Keep a list of any missing workstation/furniture parts. Submit to your vendor for replacement within a week or two after your move.	-7 to -15

8 | Utilities, Notifications and Pre-Move Details

As your target moving date gets closer, it is time to finalize the remaining details and begin notifying customers, vendors and suppliers.

Utilities and Service Providers

Contact your utility and service providers well in advance of your target moving date. Let each provider know of your intent to relocate, the timing of your move and take the necessary steps to establish service at your new location.

Check to see if there are any utilities or services that you don't currently have, but will need in the new location. For instance, if the landlord pays for utilities in your current space, but you will be responsible for these services in your new space, be sure to establish the new service before you move.

A relocation is also a good time to evaluate your providers and make sure you are getting the best service available at a competitive price.

Customer, Vendor and Business Partner Notification

Prior to your move, inform your customers, vendors and business partners of your new location by preparing and sending a letter or email, similar to the example shown on the next page.

Be sure to specify any updated contact information, including changes to your phone/fax numbers, web address, email and social media accounts. A map with directions to the new space should be attached to the letter or email, if appropriate.

Customer, Vendor and Business Partner Notification Letter Example

October 1, 2015

Subject: Company Relocation

Dear Valued Customer:

We are delighted to announce that The Easton Group is relocating its office from 210 N. Capitol Boulevard, to a new location at 3180 Creekside Drive in the Creekside Business Park. The new facility is located approximately 3 miles away from our current location and is conveniently situated near the interstate and the airport.

We will close our office Friday, November 6th at 5:00 p.m. to begin the moving process and will re-open at our new location Monday, November 9th at 8:00 a.m.

Please be assured that this move will not affect our continued business operations and quality of service. Our website, email, and telephones, will be fully operational during the moving process and you will not experience any delays in service during this time.

Please update your records with our new contact information:

Physical Location Address
The Easton Group
3180 Creekside Drive
Suite 121
Philadelphia, PA 19102
(800) 728-6100

Mailing Address
The Easton Group
PO Box 7801
Philadelphia, PA 19102

Our other contact information will remain the same:

Website: www.theeastongroup.com
Email: support@theeastongroup.com
Facebook: www.facebook.com/TheEastonGroup
LinkedIn: www.linkedin.com/company/the-easton-group
Twitter: @TheEastonGroup

As a valued customer we thank you for taking the time to update your records. Thank you for your continued business and please feel free to contact us at 800-728-6100 with any questions. We look forward to working with you in the future.

Sincerely,

Taylor Jacobs

Signage

Determine your signage needs at the new location and contract with a sign company for design, production and installation. Specific signage needs are part of the lease negotiation process and the type, location and any restrictions on signage should be in the lease agreement. Your lease will also dictate which party pays for the cost of signage. Regardless of the responsible party, it is likely that the final design will need to be approved by both tenant and landlord.

Stationery and Supplies

Inventory all of your printed materials that reference your location. In addition to stationery, envelopes and business cards, remember to review other collateral materials such as brochures, ad slicks, invoices, receipts and any forms your business uses. Decide which items will need to be updated and schedule the printing.

You can start the process of determining what needs to be printed and in what quantities early; however, do not authorize the printing until as close as possible to your moving date. It is not uncommon for landlords, municipalities or the post office to require a last-minute change in the suite number prior to issuance of the Certificate of Occupancy.

If you have any digital file templates for items such as letterhead, fax cover sheets, memos, etc., these will need to be updated as well.

Website and Social Media

Schedule the contact information on your website to update on the day of your move. Remember to amend all pages that show your address, including pages with a locator map or directions to your office. Review company social media accounts and arrange to have each site updated on or immediately after the day of your move. Send out a reminder to employees to update their own v-card, email signature, LinkedIn profile and any other social media or professional online presence that is applicable.

Office Contents and/or Personal Property Insurance

Review your personal property and office contents coverage with your insurance agent. If you have added furnishings and equipment over the years or plan to purchase items for the new office, schedule a visit with your insurance agent to determine if any additional coverage is required. Confirm that you are covered for all office contents and equipment including computers, furnishings and documents. Your policy should protect against theft, accidental loss and damage.

Janitorial and Building Maintenance Services

Review your lease to see if you or the landlord is responsible for janitorial services and building maintenance. Maintenance items your company may be responsible for include window cleaning, heating and air conditioning systems, parking lot re-surfacing, landscaping and snow removal. Contract for any services that are the tenant's responsibility. If you have live plants in your office, consider hiring a vendor to provide regular watering and care to maintain the health and appearance of the foliage.

Employee Access and Parking

Make a list of each employee and what their specific needs will be for building access. Key cards and fobs can be programmed with different levels of access based on individual security status. The landlord or property manager will typically provide and program the required cards or fobs. If the building utilizes traditional door locks, request the required number of keys from the property manager.

If your new location has access-controlled or monitored parking, determine the number of passes or permits required and request them from the parking authority. Notify employees of any rules they will need to abide by regarding building security and parking.

Create an Office Moving Map

Prior to packing, define a system for identifying each space in your new office. For small offices with a handful of employees, naming areas, i.e., Reception, Conference Room, President's office, is fine. Larger offices will find it is much easier to use numbers starting at a corner or the main entrance and working your way around the space, numbering areas in order. Whichever system you choose, identify each room or area on a copy of your new space plan with its name or number. This becomes your master moving map, and shows the delivery locations for everything that is being moved into the new space.

Moving Insurance and Pre-Move Documentation

Despite the best laid plans, accidents can and will happen. It is impossible to expect all of your furnishings and equipment will arrive at your new office in the same condition they left your old office. Damage can also occur at both locations including in building lobbies, elevators and hallways. Fortunately, having the proper insurance coverage can protect your company against damage or losses that may occur.

Hopefully you have selected a moving company that carries adequate insurance coverage and you have updated your business policies based on recommendations from your insurance agent. With good documentation, you will be well-positioned to reduce liability and be fairly compensated in the event of damage or loss.

Proper documentation includes taking photos of your furnishings and equipment prior to your target moving date. You should also photograph your current space and your new space, paying close attention to the walls, flooring, doorways and elevators. These areas are most susceptible to damage during a move.

Update your office inventory list and make sure that the list includes each item that will be moved. Your photos and inventory list will be used after the relocation to confirm damage or missing items and will be critical for an insurance claim.

Details Unique to Your Business

Because each business is unique, you may find that some issues arise which are not covered here. Keep a record of such items, listing the task and the approximate timeframe for completion. If this is something that can be delegated, make a note of who will be performing the task. This will help to keep any other miscellaneous items from falling through the cracks.

Considerations

Utilities, Notifications and Pre-Move Details

- *Consider your signage needs*, including building exterior, lobby directory, entry door and monument signage. A sign designer can prepare mock-ups that you can use to get landlord approval, if required, before ordering.

- *If you plan to advertise in the phone book, contact your local phone directory publisher* to determine their listing and advertising deadlines.

- *Verify how many keys and/or access cards* will be required and order from the property manager or landlord. (Most landlords do not allow tenants to duplicate keys.) The landlord may also request a list of employees who have keys and/or after-hours access.

- *To help generate enthusiasm, post a photo or elevation of the building* and space plan with paint, wall covering and carpet samples. If the new facility is local, take the employees on a tour. Be sure that everyone feels included and part of the process.

- *Double-check with your vendors* to make sure your account representatives are also aware of your relocation. Your change-of-address cards may go to your vendor's accounting department, and individual account representatives and delivery personnel may be unaware you have moved.

- *If moving after hours or on a weekend,* check to see that the building will be open (if you don't already have a master key) and whether or not the heating and cooling system will be in operation. Also, determine if there are any requirements for additional building security during after-hours moves.

- ***Check to see if the landlord*** or property manager requires you to use a specific entrance for your move. Landlords occasionally prefer that a side or rear loading door is used rather than the building's main lobby entrance.

- ***If you will be utilizing a freight elevator in the building,*** determine if you will need a key. If so, make arrangements to get the key prior to the move.

- ***Permits may be required*** if streets will be blocked during the move. Contact your municipality or the local police department if you think this will be an issue.

- ***Make arrangements to have pizza*** or sandwiches brought in on moving day. This will serve two purposes: It will show your appreciation for the employee's efforts and it will maximize the efficiency of the move by keeping the staff on-site during mealtimes. Breakfast items for those that arrive early are also a nice touch.

- ***Protective coverings for walls, floors*** and elevators should be used where needed, in both your current and new locations.

- ***Schedule a walk-through with your moving vendor*** to assess any damage to furniture and equipment before and after the move.

Action Steps

Utilities, Notifications and Pre-Move Details

	Timing Prior to Move
	(in days)
☐ Determine whether building provided security will be adequate for your needs. If not, arrange for security vendors to tour your facility and submit proposals.	120
☐ Notify landlord of how you would like your company's name and/or logo to appear on the building monument, lobby directory and door sign, if applicable.	120
☐ Obtain estimates for any signage needs that will not be provided by the landlord.	120
☐ Order building and office signage, if applicable.	90
☐ Order individual employee nameplates for office and workstations, if needed.	90
☐ Review security system proposals, order and arrange for installation of security system.	90
☐ Contact your insurance agent to make appropriate changes to your coverage. Consider getting quotes from other insurance vendors.	75
☐ Arrange for internal maintenance and cleaning service at the new facility, if not provided by the landlord.	75
☐ Arrange for any external building maintenance that your company will be responsible for at the new facility; such as snow removal, landscaping, etc.	75
☐ Arrange for trash pick-up and recycling at new location, if not provided by the landlord.	75
☐ Assign individual offices and workstations. Add names to your space plan, this will become your "master moving map" for moving day.	60

		Timing Prior to Move
		(in days)
☐	Determine what staff members will be on-site for moving day to direct moving vendors.	60
☐	Order new stationery, envelopes, business cards, labels, invoices, checks, bank deposit slips, brochures, sales materials, etc.	30
☐	Notify utility and service companies of disconnection and connection dates. Disconnection should occur just after mover's loading time, and new connection should occur just before mover's delivery time. Sometimes overlapping by a day is necessary.	30
☐	Notify customers, vendors and business partners of your new location.	30
☐	Send change of address notification to banks, insurance carriers, credit card companies, newspapers, magazines, associations, clubs, vendors and customers, etc.	14
☐	Order keys and access cards from landlord or property manager.	14
☐	Notify post office of new address and arrange for mail forwarding.	14
☐	Update the address and phone numbers of any document templates, such as letterhead, fax coversheets, memos, etc.	14
☐	Create a map showing driving instructions to the new location and distribute to employees.	7
☐	Take photos of furnishings, equipment and traffic-areas at your current and new locations, for insurance claim purposes.	3
☐	Order beverages, lunch and snacks to be on hand on moving day for the on-site moving team.	3
☐	Update company website and social media accounts with new contact information.	1

		Timing Prior to Move
		(in days)
☐	Distribute new keys and/or access cards to employees.	1
☐	Empty and clean refrigerator and any other appliances at the current location.	1
☐	Post the "master moving map" at the new location.	1
☐	Post individual labels on offices and common areas per the "master moving map." (i.e., reception area, break room, office #1, office #2, etc.)	1
☐	Protect main moving paths in current and new facilities with heavy-duty plastic. Be sure to tape down edges to avoid a tripping hazard.	1

9 | Packing and Unpacking Office Contents

Moving a business presents unique challenges for packing, particularly when it comes to desk contents, files and supplies. Efficiently relocating these items requires the correct type and quantity of boxes and the proper moving supplies, including packing tape, protective wrap and labeling materials.

Most moving companies sell moving materials, and many can also do the packing and unpacking for you. The moving company proposals should include pricing on supplies and packing services to assist you in deciding whether to utilize the mover for these items or to obtain supplies and perform packing and unpacking duties on your own.

Before purchasing boxes and moving supplies, double-check with your moving company to make sure these materials were not included in their bid. Also confirm if any items can remain in filing cabinets or desks. Some moving companies are able to move furnishings with files in place, which will save significantly on moving supplies and packing time. Of course, if new furniture has been purchased and the current furniture is not being relocated, everything will need to be packed.

Moving Supplies

You can protect your valuable business content by using strong, sturdy boxes that are designed for moving files, manuals, binders, office equipment, supplies and employee personal items. Using quality moving boxes will save time and reduce frustration. Moving boxes are available in the following typical sizes:

File boxes, with lid – 10" x 12" x 15"
- files
- personal items

Small boxes – 12" x 12" x 16"
- heavy items
- manuals
- books

Medium boxes – 18" x 18" x 16"
- most efficient size
- works best for light- to medium-weight items

Large boxes – 18" x 18" x 24"
- large, light-weight items

Wardrobe boxes – 24" x 24" x 40" (These boxes come with a 24" removable bar, typically not needed for office use)
- perfect for over-sized, bulky items, such as
- banners,
- projector screens,
- flip charts

Picture boxes – 60" x 60" x 4"
- ideal for framed artwork and
- mirrors
- flat-screen monitors

You'll also need packing tape and protective wrap. The ideal tape for sealing moving boxes is acrylic shipping tape on a roll. Choose tape that is 2" wide with a minimum thickness of 2.2 millimeters. Tape dispensers will make the job much easier; plan on having several available to be shared between employees.

Professional movers rely on bubble wrap for its lightweight and superior cushioning properties. Bubble wrap comes in 12" widths and is available on rolls of various lengths. Have plenty on hand for protecting small office equipment and fragile items.

The following chart shows the quantity of boxes and supplies typically required for each type of space in a typical office. If your needs are unique, adjust the sizes and quantities to suit your requirements.

Quantities for Moving Boxes and Supplies

	Small Office	Executive Office	Conference Room	Cubicle	Break Room	Supply Room
File boxes	4-6	6-8	0	2-4	0	0
Small boxes	4	4	2	2	4	8
Medium boxes	2	6	2	2	8	10
Large boxes	2	4	2	1	8	10
Wardrobe boxes	0	0	0	0	0	2
Bubble wrap	100 ft. roll	175 ft. roll	100 ft. roll	30 ft. roll	175 ft. roll	175 ft. roll
Tape	.5 roll	1 roll	.5 roll	.5 roll	2 rolls	3 rolls
Markers	1	1	1	1	2	2

Moving supplies, whether provided by the moving company or purchased on your own, should be delivered to your current office at least 30 days prior to the moving date. If you have a large quantity of items to relocate, supplies can be delivered considerably earlier and employees can begin packing non-essentials well in advance of the move. Supplies and desk items that are used on a daily basis can be packed a day or two before the move.

Labeling Moving Boxes

Instruct employees to mark each box with the name of the person who packed it, the name or number of the space it is being delivered to, a brief description of the contents, and if special handling is required. It is also helpful to number the boxes for each office or area, including the total quantity used for each office, e.g. 1 of 5, 2 of 5, etc. Boxes that contain information or critical project files that may be needed immediately after the move should be marked as priority to indicate that they should be opened first.

Office Packing Tips

Strategic packing using an efficient and organized system will ensure minimal disruption and faster unpacking after the move. Remind employees that moving provides an opportunity to reevaluate equipment and supply needs, to archive outdated files and to purge items and documents that are no longer needed.

Filing Cabinets

Determine your company's policy for document storage and if you don't already have rules in place, create an archiving policy stating how long files need to be kept, when they can be moved to off-site storage and when they can be discarded (shredded/recycled). Your policy should include rules for digital data as well as physical files.

Once you know what needs to be moved and what doesn't, all files should be sorted and placed in one of the following categories:

- Take to the new office

- Move to off-site storage

- Shred/recycle

Place files that will be moved in appropriately-sized file boxes and label carefully to maintain organizational structure when unpacked. If multiple boxes are needed for a single drawer, label each box as 1 of 4, 2 of 4, etc., in the same order as the drawer content.

Pack each box with enough files to fill it completely without over stuffing. A full file box will keep the contents from shifting during the move, insuring that contents aren't shuffled.

Desks and Credenzas

Employees should be responsible for their own offices or cubicles, unless the moving company will be packing these items. Each desk drawer should be emptied and contents sorted. Unused items can be disposed of or donated; the objective is to only take what is needed to the new office. File drawers in desks and credenzas should be handled similarly to the section on filing cabinets above.

Pack pencil drawer items and small office supplies in small- to medium-sized boxes. Gather similar small or awkward shaped items, such as pens, pencils and scissors, wrap or roll in a sheet of bubble wrap, and secure with tape. This technique will group like items together keeping the contents of each box organized. Place large, heavier items, such as packages of stationery and reference materials, at the bottom; stack smaller items on top.

Desktop personal items, awards and photos should be bubble wrapped, taped and placed in boxes. Fit several wrapped pieces, snugly, yet comfortably, in each box, depending on item size. Be sure to mark these boxes as fragile.

Pack wall art in four-part picture/mirror boxes designed for this purpose. These boxes are typically 3-1/2 to 4 inches deep and can accommodate up to a 40 inch by 60 inch piece of artwork.

Bookshelves

Place similarly sized books in small boxes to manage the weight of each box. Slide books into boxes with their spines facing the box top. This orientation will better protect your books and make unpacking easier.

Decorative bookshelf items, awards, etc. should be packed individually in a sheet of bubble wrap and taped. Wrapped pieces can be grouped together and packed similarly to desktop personal items.

Office Equipment

Large office equipment and computers should be moved by professionals, but smaller pieces can be packed and moved by employees, if desired. Bubble wrap equipment and place in an appropriately-sized box. Fill any gaps in the box with additional sheets of bubble wrap to secure. If power cords were removed, label and place in the same box.

Communicating Packing and Moving Instructions to Employees

Using the template on the following page, send an email to employees a few months prior to moving day with information on when the moving boxes and packing materials will be delivered. Include details on the moving dates and any other pertinent details.

Relocation and Packing Instruction Letter to Employees

October 15, 2016

To All Staff Members:

Subject: Arrangements for our Office Move

The move to our new offices is scheduled to take place beginning on November 6th.

In order for things to run smoothly during the move, everyone will need to clean out their own desk and pack up the contents in boxes prior to leaving the office on Friday the 6th. Boxes will be provided to you in your work area this week. Please remove everything from the walls of your work area and pack those items in the boxes along with all of your other belongings and work materials.

Please make sure that you clearly mark your first and last name on the top and sides of each box. Number each box in sequence and make a note of your total box count for later cross-checking that all of your material has been received. Marker pens will be provided for this when your boxes are delivered. If you have valuables among your personal belongings, you should take them home with you before the move.

On the morning of the 9th, you will find your boxes in your designated office area at the new building. Please unpack your boxes and put things away as soon as practical. In addition to moving into new office space, we are also installing an updated phone system. A training session will be held at 10:00 a.m. on November 9th to get everyone up and running on the new system as soon as possible. The office manager will be emailing a calendar invite for the training session to each employee.

I am confident that if everyone does their part and follows the plan, we can minimize any disruptions and have a successful relocation to the new office space.

This is an exciting change for our company and I thank you in advance for your cooperation.

Taylor Jacobs

Considerations

Packing and Unpacking Office Contents

- ***Save time and money by only packing*** and moving what you will need in the new location; carefully purge files and donate or dispose of outdated items before your relocation date.

- ***Consider the size and weight of item***s when selecting moving boxes. Properly sized boxes will be easier to transport and will better protect your office contents.

- ***Use high-quality, heavy-duty boxes*** whenever possible. Durable boxes can be stacked higher on moving cart, reducing the number of trips between the office and moving truck and can lower the overall cost of the move.

- ***If employees have personal and/or valuable items, consider asking them to pack*** and move these things separately to limit damage or potential loss.

Action Steps
Packing and Unpacking Office Contents

		Timing Prior to Move
		(in days)
☐	Determine if the moving company will be providing boxes and moving supplies, or if you will be purchasing separately.	150
☐	If you will be responsible for boxes and supplies, determine quantities required and place order.	120
☐	Schedule delivery of moving materials to arrive 2 to 3 months prior to your moving date (whether coming from the moving company or an office supplies vendor).	90
☐	Communicate packing and moving instructions to employees.	90
☐	Begin packing non-essential items, archived files and office supplies.	60
☐	Pack remaining office content except for current work files and critical items needed up until the moving date.	14
☐	Employees to pack personal items.	7
☐	Pack equipment that does not typically get daily use (binding machines, laminators, etc.)	7
☐	Wrap and box telephone handsets and other daily use equipment.	1
☐	Final packing of current work files and essential items.	1
☐	Unpack current work files and essential items.	-1
☐	Unpack remaining boxes.	-2 to -7

10 | Relocation Wrap-Up

There are still many tasks to be completed once your moving day has come and gone. Wrapping up these details quickly will help maintain morale and ensure that business activities continue uninterrupted to the extent possible.

Post-Move Review

When the move is complete, check the delivery and condition of each item on the inventory list. Make a list of any missing or damaged items and take photos, if applicable. Review list and photos with a representative from the moving company, preferably on the day of the move, or as soon as possible afterward, and initiate the claims process. Claims typically need to be filed within a specific timeframe – check with the applicable vendor to confirm claim time limitations. Keep copies of any submitted claim forms and follow up with the moving company to make sure the claim is resolved in a timely manner.

Evaluate Premises

Once the boxes are unpacked and everyone is settled into the new office, perform a final walkthrough to determine whether the vendors involved in the move completed their tasks as planned. When performing the walkthrough, pay close attention to these areas:

- Construction

- IT/Telecommunications issues

- Workstation assembly

Any damage or incomplete work should be brought to the immediate attention of the appropriate vendor. Follow up to be sure all issues are addressed to your satisfaction.

In the 30 to 60 days after your move, continue to evaluate your premises to be sure that everything meets your expectations. Run a thorough test of the heating and cooling system, regardless of the season, to make sure both are performing properly. Now is the time to bring any concerns to the property manager or landlord.

Keep a record of these conversations, including the property manager or landlord's response and any actions taken. If the complaint is for something other than a minor issue, it is a good idea to put it in writing; send a letter or an email rather than making a phone call.

Plan an Open House

Consider scheduling an open house or after-move party within 60 to 90 days of your relocation. There are several benefits of this type of event; of course it's a great way to showcase your new space with your clients and the business community, but it's also a motivation tool to get the boxes unpacked and everything in its place sooner rather than later.

Building Information

As soon as possible after the move, create a Building Information sheet, example on next page. This document includes information about the building's ownership, the property management company and appropriate contacts and phone numbers for maintenance personnel. Keep a copy of the Building Information sheet with your lease and consider posting it in your break room, in case of an emergency.

Building Information - Example

Building Information	
Building Name:	Presidio Center
Address:	3180 Creekside Dr. Suite 121 Philadelphia, PA
Leasing Agent:	Charlotte Canfield
Agent's Phone Number:	267-461-4966
Leasing Company:	Horizon Commercial Real Estate
Leasing Company Address:	210 Broadway Suite 111 Philadelphia, PA
Property Management Company:	Commercial Properties
Property Management Contact:	Michael Robertson
Property Management Phone Number:	267-630-2940
Emergency/After-Hours Number:	267-630-3000
Building Owner:	The Castle Group
Owner's Mailing Address:	One Commerce Centre Suite 400 Dallas, TX
Other Important Information/Contacts:	Cleaning Company - Smith's Janitorial 267-342-5007, Jane Smith, Manager Electrician - Slater Electric 267-345-6210, Mark Griffith

Considerations

Relocation Wrap-Up

- *After the movers have finished, provide a welcome package* to employees. The package could include a company telephone directory reflecting new extensions, a map of the area and local amenities (check with leasing agent to see if they have a map that can be copied), and a welcoming gift or memento of the move, perhaps an "I Survived The Move" paperweight or t-shirt.

- *Review emergency exits and evacuation plan* with employees. Post emergency numbers and other important contact information in the breakroom and common areas. Important phone numbers should include your security system provider and the building property manager.

- *Be sure to file any damage or insurance claims* as soon as possible. Follow-up regularly until each claim is completed.

- *Remember to fully evaluate your heating and cooling system* regardless of the current season. If you wait until the next season to raise or lower the thermostat and there is a problem, it may be too late to have the cost of repairs covered by the landlord.

- *Consider celebrating your move with an open house.* Many businesses have received invaluable recognition and free press by inviting the local Chamber of Commerce to perform a ribbon-cutting ceremony.

Action Steps

Relocation Wrap-Up

		Timing Prior to Move
		(in days)
☐	Check carefully for any damaged or missing furniture or items, assess former and new locations for damage, notify moving company if a claim needs to be filed.	-1
☐	Collect keys, access cards and parking passes for former office space from employees and return them to the landlord or property manager.	-1
☐	Prepare Building Information sheet; keep in your lease file and post a copy in one of your common areas.	-1
☐	Post and review emergency exits and evacuation plan.	-1
☐	Return to former office to pick up mail and/or packages that may not have been forwarded.	-5
☐	Perform a walk-through of the new space to ensure all furnishings and equipment have been installed properly.	-7
☐	If anything is not completed satisfactorily, contact the appropriate vendor for remedy.	-7
☐	Schedule an "after the move" meeting with the relocation team to debrief and address any questions or concerns.	-7
☐	Begin to make open house arrangements, if you intend to hold such an event.	-14

Appendix A | Master Timeline

Chapter			Timing Prior to Move (in months)
1	☐	Appoint a relocation coordinator and/or relocation team.	12 – 14
1	☐	Schedule the prospective moving day, knowing that this may be a moving target until an office space is selected and other factors are determined.	12 – 14
1	☐	Determine your relocation budget including estimates for professional advisory fees, moving expenses, and the cost of new furnishings and equipment.	12 – 14
2	☐	Review what works and what doesn't work in your current space with your relocation and advisory teams.	11 – 12
2	☐	Interview and select a commercial real estate agent.	11 – 12
2	☐	Calculate the amount of square footage your business requires.	11 – 12
2	☐	With your commercial real estate agent's help, if using, develop your facility/site criteria, including all requirements that need to be met in your new location.	11 – 12

Chapter			Timing Prior to Move
2	☐	Contact landlords/real estate agents to set up appointments for building property tours. (If you are using a broker, he or she will do this for you.)	11 – 12
2	☐	Your commercial real estate agent, if using, will identify properties in your market which best meet your requirements and provide you with a property availability report.	10 – 12
2	☐	Tour selected buildings, take detailed notes.	9 – 11
2	☐	Narrow alternatives to a short list of two or three choices.	9 – 11
2	☐	Have an architect/space planner create test-fit floor plans for short-listed properties.	9 – 11
2	☐	Review test-fit floor plans, provide feedback to architect/space planner.	9 – 11
2	☐	Develop an RFP based on your needs.	8 – 10
2	☐	Deliver the RFP to the landlords of the top two or three buildings you have chosen to pursue.	8 – 10
2	☐	Receive RFP responses from landlords.	8 – 10
2	☐	Select most suitable property for your business, request lease from landlord.	6 – 8
2	☐	Have a decision-maker from your company, your commercial real estate agent, if using, and your real estate attorney review the lease.	6 – 8
2	☐	Ensure any negotiated lease revisions have been incorporated into the final lease document.	6 – 8

Chapter			Timing Prior to Move
2	☐	Finalize space plan and interior color selections, construction should begin on space as soon as lease has been signed and final space plan has been approved.	6 – 8
2	☐	Request final lease documents, sign lease.	5 – 7
2	☐	Prepare and send employee notification memo/email to all staff members and employees of your company.	5 – 7

			Timing Prior to Move (in days)
7	☐	Determine whether any furnishings need to be replaced, upgraded or purchased.	210
7	☐	Select vendors to interview, evaluate product lines, and review budget requirements, if new furniture is required.	210
3	☐	Contact property managers at current and new locations to determine any restrictions on timing of your move. (Time of day restrictions, specific exits/elevators, etc.)	180
3	☐	Determine target moving date.	180
3	☐	Inventory furniture and equipment. Identify which items will be moved.	180
3	☐	Create moving plan with detailed inventory list, location and scheduling information.	180
5	☐	Inventory existing computers, server and telecommunications equipment.	180
7	☐	Have each furniture vendor provide an office furniture layout and proposal.	180

Chapter			Timing Prior to Move
4	☐	Schedule three movers to perform a site visit of your current location and to prepare estimates based on your moving plan and inventory list.	150
5	☐	Identify current telecommunication usage and future needs.	150
5	☐	Decide whether to relocate your existing server(s), computers and telephone system or if new equipment needs to be purchased.	150
5	☐	If a new telephone system, server equipment, or computers are required, make arrangements to interview vendors and begin the selection process.	150
6	☐	Determine whether any equipment needs to be upgraded or replaced.	150
7	☐	Review furniture proposals, check references and select a furniture vendor.	150
7	☐	Based on your furniture vendor's layout and proposal, determine your actual furnishing needs and place order with vendor.	150
9	☐	Determine if the moving company will be providing boxes and moving supplies, or if you will be purchasing separately.	150
4	☐	Review moving company estimates, verify each company meets licensing and insurance requirements.	120
5	☐	Review phone system and new equipment proposals, select vendors and order equipment.	120
5	☐	Establish the network and data cabling requirements at your new facility, with the assistance of your IT consultant.	120

Chapter			Timing Prior to Move
5	☐	Select three voice and network cabling companies to review the space plan and tour the new facility to determine your cabling needs. Have each company submit a proposal for the services you'll require.	120
6	☐	Make arrangements to interview office equipment vendors and begin the selection process, if new equipment is needed.	120
6	☐	Review office equipment vendor proposals, select equipment vendors.	120
8	☐	Determine whether building provided security will be adequate for your needs. If not, arrange for security vendors to tour your facility and submit proposals.	120
8	☐	Notify landlord of how you would like your company's name and/or logo to appear on the building monument, lobby directory and door sign, if applicable.	120
8	☐	Obtain estimates for any signage needs that will not be provided by the landlord.	120
9	☐	If you will be responsible for boxes and supplies, determine quantities required and place order.	120
4	☐	Contact references provided by each moving company.	100
4	☐	Select moving company, schedule moving date.	100
5	☐	Select three long distance providers to submit quotes for their services. (Remember to check with your new landlord on the availability of shared telecommunication services.)	90
5	☐	Choose voice and data cabling vendor. Schedule installation to occur 30 days before your move-in date. Coordinate with landlord and/or building contractor.	90

Chapter			Timing Prior to Move
6	☐	Place orders for new office equipment and set delivery on or before your move-in date.	90
6	☐	If existing copiers and/or printers will be moved, contact vendors to schedule removal of toner and determine whether they would prefer to move the equipment. If so, schedule moving date with vendors.	90
8	☐	Order building and office signage, if applicable.	90
8	☐	Order individual employee nameplates for office and workstations, if needed.	90
8	☐	Review security system proposals, order and arrange for installation of security system.	90
9	☐	Schedule delivery of moving materials to arrive 2 to 3 months prior to your moving date (whether coming from the moving company or an office supplies vendor).	90
9	☐	Communicate packing and moving instructions to employees.	90
5	☐	Review long distance proposals, select provider and order long distance service.	75
5	☐	Order or set up the transfer of phone and fax numbers.	75
5	☐	Contact all carriers and internet service providers (ISP's) with information on your new location and your anticipated move date.	75
8	☐	Contact your insurance agent to make appropriate changes to your coverage. Consider getting quotes from other insurance vendors.	75

Chapter			Timing Prior to Move
8	☐	Arrange for internal maintenance and cleaning service at the new facility, if not provided by the landlord.	75
8	☐	Arrange for any external building maintenance that your company will be responsible for at the new facility; such as snow removal, landscaping, etc.	75
8	☐	Arrange for trash pick-up and recycling at new location, if not provided by the landlord.	75
5	☐	Make arrangements for phones to be operational on moving day. If necessary, have phones forwarded to temporary locations or cell phones during the actual move.	60
6	☐	Check with your security system vendor to determine if components at your current location can be relocated, if applicable.	60
7	☐	If moving any existing workstations, schedule your furniture vendor to disassemble at your old location and reassemble at your new location.	60
8	☐	Assign individual offices and workstations. Add names to your space plan, this will become your "master moving map" for moving day.	60
8	☐	Determine what staff members will be on-site for moving day to direct moving vendors.	60
9	☐	Begin packing non-essential items, archived files and office supplies.	60
6	☐	If you have bottled water, coffee service and/or vending machines, arrange for their respective vendors to relocate this equipment.	45
5	☐	Have cabling vendor begin installation at new facility.	30

Chapter			Timing Prior to Move
5	☐	Confirm your network consultant is available to shut down your network immediately prior to your actual move and to restore the network at the new location as soon as feasible.	30
7	☐	Schedule delivery and assembly of new furniture, if applicable, preferably prior to moving day.	30
7	☐	Plan for disposal of furniture that will not be needed. Consider reselling or donating.	30
8	☐	Order new stationery, envelopes, business cards, labels, invoices, checks, bank deposit slips, brochures, sales materials, etc.	30
8	☐	Notify utility and service companies of disconnection and connection dates. Disconnection should occur just after mover's loading time, and new connection should occur just before mover's delivery time. Sometimes overlapping by a day is necessary.	30
8	☐	Notify customers, vendors and business partners of your new location.	30
8	☐	Send change of address notification to banks, insurance carriers, credit card companies, newspapers, magazines, associations, clubs, vendors and customers, etc.	14
8	☐	Order keys and access cards from landlord or property manager.	14
8	☐	Notify post office of new address and arrange for mail forwarding.	14
8	☐	Update the address and phone numbers of any document templates, such as letterhead, fax coversheets, memos, etc.	14

Chapter			Timing Prior to Move
9	☐	Pack remaining office content except for current work files and critical items needed up until the moving date.	14
8	☐	Create a map showing driving instructions to the new location and distribute to employees.	7
9	☐	Employees to pack personal items.	7
9	☐	Pack equipment that does not typically get daily use (binding machines, laminators, etc.)	7
5	☐	Test all network and phone drops as soon as cabling vendor completes installation.	5
5	☐	Install new phone system at new location, if applicable.	5
5	☐	Assign employee phone numbers or extensions.	5
8	☐	Take photos of furnishings, equipment and traffic-areas at your current and new locations, for insurance claim purposes.	3
8	☐	Order beverages, lunch and snacks to be on hand on moving day for the on-site moving team.	3
5	☐	Back up all company data. Require employees using personal computers to back up their own hard drives.	1
5	☐	Have your network consultant on hand near the end of the day immediately prior to your move to shut down the network. Make sure all employees have plenty of notice and are aware of the shutdown date and time.	1
7	☐	Furniture vendor to dismantle existing workstations to be moved.	1

Chapter			Timing Prior to Move
8	☐	Update company website and social media accounts with new contact information.	1
8	☐	Distribute new keys and/or access cards to employees.	1
8	☐	Empty and clean refrigerator and any other appliances at the current location.	1
8	☐	Post the "master moving map" at the new location.	1
8	☐	Post individual labels on offices and common areas per the "master moving map." (i.e., reception area, break room, office #1, office #2, etc.)	1
8	☐	Protect main moving paths in current and new facilities with heavy-duty plastic. Be sure to tape down edges to avoid a tripping hazard.	1
9	☐	Wrap and box telephone handsets and other daily use equipment.	1
9	☐	Final packing of current work files and essential items.	1
5	☐	Restore and test the network as soon as computer equipment is installed at the new location.	0
6	☐	Take delivery of copiers and printers at new location; verify that the toner has been replaced and that the equipment is operational. Make sure you have two extra toner cartridges on hand for each piece of equipment. Place order for additional supplies, if necessary.	0
5	☐	Review telephone system programming and routing, make any necessary changes.	-1
6	☐	Verify that coffee service equipment, water cooler and vending machines have been delivered and are operational. Ensure there are adequate levels of supplies for each (coffee, water bottles, disposable cups, etc.).	-1

Chapter			Timing Prior to Move
7	☐	Furniture vendor to re-assemble workstations in new location.	-1
9	☐	Unpack current work files and essential items.	-1
10	☐	Check carefully for any damaged or missing furniture or items, assess former and new locations for damage, notify moving company if a claim needs to be filed.	-1
10	☐	Collect keys, access cards and parking passes for former office space from employees and return them to the landlord or property manager.	-1
10	☐	Prepare Building Information sheet; keep in your lease file and post a copy in one of your common areas.	-1
10	☐	Post and review emergency exits and evacuation plan.	-1
5	☐	Hold training session for employees to learn new phone system, if applicable. Have phone system representative on hand to answer questions and assist with any issues that have come up.	-1 to -5
7	☐	Verify that all systems furniture is assembled and configured per the vendor's proposal.	-2
9	☐	Unpack remaining boxes.	-2 to -7
10	☐	Return to former office to pick up mail and/or packages that may not have been forwarded.	-5
10	☐	Perform a walk-through of the new space to ensure all furnishings and equipment have been installed properly.	-7
10	☐	Schedule an "after the move" meeting with the relocation team to debrief and address any questions or concerns.	-7

Chapter			Timing Prior to Move
10	☐	Schedule an "after the move" meeting with the relocation team to debrief and address any questions or concerns.	-7
7	☐	Keep a list of any missing workstation/furniture parts. Submit to your vendor for replacement within a week or two after your move.	-7 to -15
5	☐	Arrange to donate or recycle any network or telecommunications equipment that is no longer needed.	-7 to -30
6	☐	Arrange to donate or recycle obsolete equipment.	-7 to -30
10	☐	Begin to make open house arrangements, if you intend to hold such an event.	-14

Appendix B | Forms

The following pages contain templates for the forms referred to throughout this book.

As every leasing situation is unique, you may need to customize these forms to suit your particular circumstances.

Template forms include:

- Relocation Expense Budget
- Proposal Analysis
- Office Moving Inventory
- Building Information Form

Office Relocation Budget

Monthly Facility Expenses

Rent and Other Monthly Expenses	Budget	Actual	Variance ($)	Variance (%)
Rent	$	$	$	%
Insurance	$	$	$	%
Communication/Networking Fees	$	$	$	%
Utilities	$	$	$	%
Common Area Maintenance	$	$	$	%
Property Taxes	$	$	$	%
Janitorial Services	$	$	$	%
Total Rent and Other Monthly Facility Expenses	$	$	$	%

Relocation Expenses

Location & Leasing Fees	Budget	Actual	Variance ($)	Variance (%)
Attorney Fees	$	$	$	%
Architect/Space Planner	$	$	$	%
Communication/Network Consultant	$	$	$	%
Additional Tenant Improvements, not included in rent	$	$	$	%
Security Deposit	$	$	$	%
Signage (may be included as negotiated lease term)	$	$	$	%
Network Cabling	$	$	$	%
Security System, door locks, alarms, etc.	$	$	$	%
Total Leasing Fees	$	$	$	%

Moving Expenses	Budget	Actual	Variance ($)	Variance (%)
Moving Vendor	$	$	$	%
Computer Relocation Vendor	$	$	$	%
Other Moving Vendors – Equipment/Artwork, etc.	$	$	$	%
Total Moving Expenses	$	$	$	%

New Equipment/Furnishings	Budget	Actual	Variance ($)	Variance (%)
Phone System	$	$	$	%
Office Equipment, copiers, fax machines, etc.	$	$	$	%
Conferencing/Audio Visual Equipment	$	$	$	%
Computers	$	$	$	%
Furnishings	$	$	$	%
Supplies	$	$	$	%
Breakroom/kitchen appliances	$	$	$	%
Total New Equipment/Furnishings Expenses	$	$	$	%

Printing/Marketing	Budget	Actual	Variance ($)	Variance (%)
Re-print stationery, business cards, etc.	$	$	$	%
Change website and online contact info, maps	$	$	$	%
Graphic designer fees, update ad slicks, etc.	$	$	$	%
Total Printing/Marketing Expenses	$	$	$	%

| **Total Relocation Expenses** | **$** | **$** | **$** | **%** |

Proposal Analysis

Proposal Items	Tenant's Request	Landlord's Response	Decision
Premises			
Area/Sq. Ft.			
Possession and Commencement			
Occupancy Date			
Lease Term			
Rental Rate			
Security Deposit			
Tenant Improvements			
Option to Renew			
Expansion Option			
Signage			
Access			
Mechanical Systems			
Fire/Safety Systems			
Building Security			
Elevators			
Parking			

Proposal Analysis, cont.

Proposal Items	Tenant's Request	Landlord's Response	Decision
Additional Storage Space			
Building Ownership			
Property Management			
Building Amenities			
Standard Lease			
References			

Office Moving Inventory

Company and Location Information

	Current Location	New Location
Company Name:		Target Moving Date:
Building Address		
Suite Number		
City, State ZIP		
Size (square feet)		
Special Instructions/ Building or Location Challenges		

	Company Contact	Moving Company Contact
Contact		
Contact Phone		
Contact Email		

Inventory List

Item	Description	Quantity	Notes
Desks	Executive and task desks		
Credenzas	Secondary desk/worksurface		
Bookshelves	Book or storage		
Cubicles	Systems furniture		
Task Chairs	Chairs on wheels or rollers		
Conference Tables	Large or small		
Conference Chairs	Fixed chairs, arm or side		
Filing Cabinets	2-drawer and 4-drawer		
Desktop Computers	Desktop or tower		
Monitors	Computer monitors and TV's		
Copiers/Printers/Faxes	Multi-function machines, plotters		
A/V Equipment	Projection equipment, screens		
Telephone Handsets	Telephone equipment, handsets and headsets		
Other Equipment	Postage meters, plotters, scanners, etc.		
Office Supplies	General quantities of supplies		

Moving Supplies

Supply Type	Description	Quantity	Notes
File Boxes	10" x 12" x 15" or similar		
Small Boxes	12" x 12" x 16" or similar		
Medium Boxes	18" x 18" x 16" or similar		
Large Boxes	18" x 18" x 24" or similar		
Wardrobe Boxes	24" x 24" x 40" or similar		
Tape	2" wide, 2.2 millimeter		
Tape Dispensers	Hand-held		
Packing Materials	Bubble-wrap, paper		
Markers	Heavy-duty, black		

Vendor Requirements

Requirement	Description	Yes/No	Notes
License	Must be licensed in applicable state(s)		
Insurance	Must carry appropriate insurance for loss and damage		
Equipment	Confirm vendor has appropriate equipment for the job		

Building Information Form

Building Information
Building Name:
Address:
Leasing Agent:
Agent's Phone Number:
Leasing Company:
Leasing Company Address:
Property Management Company:
Property Management Contact:
Property Management Phone Number:
Emergency/After-Hours Number:
Building Owner:
Owner's Mailing Address:
Other Important Information/Contacts:

Appendix C | Notification Letter Templates

Use these letter templates to notify and provide pertinent information to employees, vendors and business partners of your upcoming relocation. Templates can be customized to fit your unique needs. Letters can be printed on company letterhead and sent in the mail, or transferred to an email program and sent electronically.

The following notification letters are included:

- Move Notification Letter to Employees

- Customer, Vendor, or Business Partner Move Notification Letter

- Relocation and Packing Instruction Letter to Employees

Move Notification Letter to Employees

[Date]

To: All Office Employees

From: Company President

Subject: Office Relocation

I am very pleased to announce the relocation of our company to a new facility. As a result of [Company Name]'s growth and change in office space requirements, we will be relocating our offices to [new location address].

Our move is scheduled to occur on [date of move out of current space] and we plan to be fully relocated to our new offices by [date of move in to new space]. Further instructions on planning for the move will be sent out in the upcoming weeks.

In making this decision, many aspects of our business have been considered, most importantly of which is our employees. Although some of you may have a longer commute, I believe this move will benefit all of us through continued growth and the success of [Company Name].

I look forward to working with all of you in making this move to our new space.

Customer, Vendor, or Business Partner Move Notification Letter

[Date]

Subject: Company Relocation

Dear Valued [Customer, Vendor, Business Partner],

We are delighted to announce that [company name] is relocating its office from [current location address], to a new location at [new location address]. The new facility is located approximately [# of miles or blocks] miles away from our current location and is conveniently situated near (local landmark or other amenities).

We will close our office [date] at [time] to begin the moving process and will re-open at our new location [date] at [time].

Please be assured that this move will not affect our continued business operations and quality of service. Our website, email, and telephones, will be fully operational during the moving process and you will not experience any delays in service during this time. (If this is not the case, mention that minor interruptions of service or delays may occur during the move.)

Please update your records with our new contact information:

Physical Location Address

[Company Name]
[Street Address]
[Suite Number]
[City, State ZIP]
[Phone and Fax Numbers, if there are changes]

Mailing Address

[Company Name]
[PO Box]
[City, State ZIP]

Additional contact information will remain the same:

Website: [website URL]
Email: [email address]
Facebook: [Facebook page name]
LinkedIn: [LinkedIn page name]
Twitter: [Twitter handle]

As a valued [customer, vendor, business partner] we thank you for taking the time to update your records. Thank you for your continued business and please feel free to contact us at [phone number] with any questions. We look forward to working with you in the future.

Sincerely,

Relocation and Packing Instruction Letter to Employees

[Date]

To All Staff Members:

Subject: Arrangements for our Office Move

The move to our new offices is scheduled to take place beginning on [move out date]

In order for things to run smoothly during the move, everyone will need to clean out their own desk and pack up the contents in boxes prior to leaving the office on [move out date]. Boxes will be provided to you in your work area this week. Please remove everything from the walls of your work area and pack those items in the boxes along with all of your other belongings and work materials.

Please make sure that you clearly mark your first and last name on the top and sides of each box. Number each box in sequence and make a note of your total box count for later cross-checking that all of your material has been received. Marker pens will be provided for this when your boxes are delivered. If you have valuables among your personal belongings, you should take them home with you before the move.

On the morning of [move-in date], you will find your boxes in your designated office area at the new building. Please unpack your boxes and put things away as soon as practical. In addition to moving into new office space, we are also installing an updated phone system. A training session will be held at [time] on [date] to get everyone up and running on the new system as soon as possible. The office manager will be emailing a calendar invite for the training session to each employee.

I am confident that if everyone does their part and follows the plan, we can minimize any disruptions and have a successful relocation to the new office space.

This is an exciting change for our company and I thank you in advance for your cooperation.

Karen Warner is an office relocation specialist and commercial real estate broker. She has helped hundreds of companies with their relocation objectives. In addition to *Office Relocation Planner*, Karen is also the author of *Move Your Office* and *Winning the Office Leasing Game*. Her extensive knowledge of the commercial relocation process and unique talent as a tenant representative has helped many businesses manage a smooth transition to their new location.

CPSIA information can be obtained
at www.ICGtesting.com
Printed in the USA
LVOW03s2156240416

485132LV00009B/286/P